Shoplifting

SHOPLIFTING

Charles A. Sennewald, C.P.P., C.P.O., C.M.C.
John H. Christman, C.P.P.

Butterworth–Heinemann
Boston London Oxford Singapore Sydney Toronto Wellington

Recognizing the importance of preserving what has been written, it is the policy of Butterworth–Heinemann to have the books it publishes printed on acid-free paper, and we exert our best efforts to that end.

Library of Congress Cataloging-in-Publication Data

Sennewald, Charles A., 1931–
    Shoplifting / Charles A. Sennewald and John H. Christman.
      p. cm.
    Includes bibliographical references and index.
    ISBN 0-7506-9036-4 (case bound)
    1. Shoplifting—United States. 2. Shoplifting—United States—Prevention. 3. Retail trade—United States—Security measures.
    I. Christman, John. II. Title.
    HV6658.S46 1992
    364.1′62′0973—dc20   92-3222
                                                  CIP

British Library Cataloguing in Publication Data

Sennewald, Charles A.
  Shoplifting
  I. Title II. Christman, John H.
  364.1

  ISBN 0-7506-9036-4

Butterworth–Heinemann
80 Montvale Avenue
Stoneham, MA 02180

10 9 8 7 6 5 4 3 2 1

Printed in the United States of America

Contents

Preface

In 1961 the only available retail security text was *Modern Retail Security* by Bob Curtis. It became a part of security libraries everywhere, standing alone as a reference and introduction to the industry.

In 1980, we first began collaborating on a competitive retail security book. Unfortunately, we got bogged down and the book never came together.

It wasn't until ten years later that we realized why we couldn't write a retail book, either alone or in collaboration: The vastness of subject matter and material is awesome. We came on the idea of logically dividing the overall discipline of retail security into manageable segments. This book, which exclusively addresses the issue of shoplifting, is one of four titles we hope to produce. The remaining three cover topics such as employee dishonesty, "other" retailing crimes, and reducing inventory shortage and security awareness programs.

This strategy of focusing on interdisciplines of retail security should provide the depth that otherwise would have to be sacrificed in a single general book. And by co-authoring the work, our collective efforts have avoided individual bias or skewing that can occur in areas that tend to allow for or demand opinions or judgment calls. The end result should reflect a comprehensive and professional reference source on each topical area.

Finally, this is our first co-authored work. Sharing a writing project is tough . . . there's a magic that makes it work. We feel we have had the good fortune to find that magic and hope this book is proof of that.

Note: Whenever legal issues are discussed in this book, it should be understood that we are not giving legal advice but simply describing generally applicable information. We urge readers to consult an attorney for advice on legal issues.

Introduction

It is probably fair to say that shoplifting—a euphemism for the theft of goods offered for sale by a store—has been a problem for those who offer goods for sale since the first merchants opened their businesses to the public. Not too long ago, helpful clerks obtained goods for the customer from behind counters and shelving. Today, the extent of the shoplifting problem has increased, and it is exacerbated by the recent trend toward self-service merchandising and modern display techniques.

COSTS OF SHOPLIFTING

Empirical evidence is difficult to accumulate, but government and private authorities agree that shoplifting is extremely costly to both merchants and consumers. Merchants are saddled with the cost of security systems, security personnel, and merchandise lost to theft; consumers pay more for the goods they purchase because some of the merchants' costs are passed on as higher prices. In 1980, shoplifting cost a family of four an estimated $250 a year in increased food prices.[1] FBI statistics show that shoplifting is the nation's fastest growing type of theft. Shoplifting cases increased 35% between 1984 and 1990.[2]

To state definitively the annual losses from shoplifting would be difficult. Losses are known only from the shoplifters who have been apprehended and prosecuted; losses from those who are never caught—the majority of shoplifters—can only be roughly estimated. Some statistics on the habits of shoplifters have been gathered:[3]

- Three percent of nonprofessional shoplifters steal every day, 14% steal every week, and 60% steal at least once a month.
- The average value of merchandise stolen by nonprofessional shoplifters for each theft is $80 to $100 from department stores, $50 to $60 from specialty stores, $8 to $18 from drug stores and supermarkets, and $2 from convenience stores.

- Professional thieves steal from $30 to $3000 per day almost every day, depending on individual needs.

As these statistics make clear, the national losses from shoplifting amount to many billions of dollars annually.

Nationwide, the estimated loss of profits resulting from shoplifting ranges from .5% to 5%, depending on the type of business, its merchandising techniques, and its effectiveness in controlling shoplifting. Consider the impact of a minimal 1% loss to a business such as a supermarket, where typical net profits run only from 1% to 2%. A loss of only 1% is fiscally damaging; higher losses usually mean financial disaster. The number of major retailers who have disappeared from the marketplace tells the story; they didn't go bankrupt because of high profits.

According to David Birchall, the director of Store Watch, Ltd., in Auckland, New Zealand, the inventory shrinkage problem and the increase in shoplifting losses are not unique to the United States.[4] He sees similar problems on his continent. Birchall's company, which contracts out anti-shoplifting security personnel and offers consulting services, reported that losses due to shoplifting exceeded $1 billion in New Zealand and Australia during 1987. As a result, his company has experienced a phenomenal rate of growth. A 1988 study by the Institute of Retail Studies at the University of Stirling, Scotland, confirms that this trend is also observed in the United Kingdom.[5]

Table 1–1 shows quite clearly the impact of shoplifting losses on retail businesses. For example, consider a supermarket with an annual sales volume of $3.5 million and a net profit of 2% ($70,000 per year). Assume that this market suffers a 2% ($70,000) annual inventory shortage. If $3.5 million generates $70,000 in profits, then the loss of $70,000 to theft (at 2% of sales) means that an equivalent amount of sales would be required to replace this shortage or loss.

Let's look at this concept another way. Consider a retailer whose business

Table 1–1 Sales required to replace losses due to theft

Annual losses	Net profit			
	2%	4.5%	7%	9%
$15,000	$750,000	$315,000	$214,300	$166,600
$70,000	$3.5 million	$1.475 million	$1 million	$777,700
$100,000	$5 million	$2.105 million	$1.428 million	$1.111 million
$300,000	$15 million	$6.315 million	$4.285 million	$3.333 million
$600,000	$30 million	$12.631 million	$8.571 million	$6.666 million
$1 million	$50 million	$21.052 million	$14.285 million	$11.111 million

Store Watch, Ltd., Auckland, New Zealand, 1987.

generates a net profit of 5%, that is, $5 in net profits on every $100 in sales. The retailer's figures would look something like this for each $100 in sales:

$100	Sale of merchandise
(50)	Cost of goods
(25)	Sales expense (salaries, etc.)
(15)	Cost of business (rent, etc.)
10	Gross profit
(5)	Taxes at 50%
5	Net profit on $100 sale

From these figures it is apparent that for every $100 lost to shoplifting, 20 additional $100 sales must be made to simply break even financially. This is an easy concept to explain to sales associates when describing the seriousness of the shoplifting problem. For every $100 dress stolen by a shoplifter, the store must sell 20 similar dresses to replace that loss. It is not until the 21st sale of a like item is made that any profit is generated. The previous twenty sales generate no profit; they simply make up for the loss of the stolen dress.

Some additional information about the prevalence of shoplifting and the habits of shoplifters is known:

- In a 1985 study by San Diego University, 42% of a random sample admitted to having shoplifted at some time during their lives; 18% said they had shoplifted during the prior 12 months.[6]
- A 1984 study by the University of Washington found that one in 11 shoppers (9%) in a Spokane, Washington, shopping center admitted shoplifting during the previous year.[7]
- Research from Shoplifters Anonymous, a national not-for-profit organization that specializes in shoplifter research and rehabilitation, shows that about 60% of nonprofessional shoplifters are habitual offenders.[8]
- On average, shoplifters are caught once for every 49 times they steal, and they are turned over to the police once every 89 times.[9]

These statistics offer graphic examples of why the national cost of shoplifting is billions of dollars.

As stated at the beginning of this chapter, *shoplifting* is a euphemism for the theft of goods offered for sale by a store. The use of this innocuous term is unfortunate because it softens the act in the offender's mind and in the public's eyes. The statistics and facts noted earlier clearly illustrate the enormous economic impact this theft has on everyone. The term *shoplifting* reduces the criminal offense of theft—make no mistake about it: Shoplifting is a crime in every jurisdiction in the United States and in all foreign countries—to something less than a crime and the shoplifter to something less than a criminal simply because a retailer is the victim. Nothing is further from the truth.

USE OF SECURITY CONTROLS

An important aspect of the shoplifting problem is the perpetual conflict within businesses of establishing sufficient security controls and presence to discourage shoplifting while simultaneously maintaining a pleasant and inviting atmosphere for customers. Retailing is a very competitive business, and all retailers spend much time and effort to devise individual approaches to entice customers into their stores and to encourage them to purchase their wares. Inappropriate or excessive use of security devices such as mirrors, cameras, and signs may be oppressive (albeit effective) and when coupled with the obvious presence of uniformed or plainclothes security personnel, are not conducive to a pleasant shopping experience.

Effective methods of controlling and deterring shoplifters do exist. However, some security techniques are appropriate—perhaps mandatory—in some situations, but totally inappropriate in other situations. For example, it is certainly appropriate to use anti-shoplifting closed-circuit television (CCTV) cameras on the selling floor, but it would be absolutely inappropriate and very likely illegal to place them in a fitting room. Similarly, it might be desirable to fasten the latest rage in teenage jeans to the selling fixture with cables to prevent shoplifting, but the customers of exclusive boutiques that sell expensive women's wear might find this procedure offensive. Where should merchants draw the line? What factors should influence their decisions? Who can they turn to for help? What can they do to minimize their losses? How can they identify and deal with shoplifters? What are their legal concerns and liabilities? Are there some things they should avoid at all costs?

GOALS OF THIS BOOK

This book was written to answer a variety of common questions about the social phenomenon of shoplifting:

Who

- Who shoplifts?
- Who can stop and detain someone for shoplifting?
- Who should be notified when a detention is made?
- Who should be referred to the police, and who should be released?
- Who has the authority to release suspected shoplifters?
- Who can be told about a suspected shoplifter's detention or arrest?

What

- What force, if any, can be used to detain suspected shoplifters?
- What kind of documentation is required when a person is detained?

- What can merchants do if a shoplifter escapes with their merchandise?
- What rights do merchants have?
- What rights do shoplifters have?
- What kind of shoplifting prevention training should regular salespeople receive?
- What can be done to make employees more aware of the shoplifting problem?
- What kind of training should security employees receive?

When

- When can suspected shoplifters be stopped?
- When can merchants accept payment for stolen goods from a shoplifter?
- When are merchants most vulnerable to shoplifters?
- When should juveniles be released to parents instead of to the authorities?
- When do merchants return evidence to stock?

Where

- Where should suspected shoplifters be questioned?
- Where can suspected shoplifters be stopped?
- Where do shoplifters most frequently conceal stolen goods?
- Where do shoplifters often secrete goods while inside the store?
- Where should evidence and records of shoplifting incidents be stored?

How

- How should suspected shoplifters be approached?
- How can nonsecurity employees best prevent, discourage, or "burn" (deter) suspected shoplifters?
- How can merchants prevent injuries when making arrests?
- How can merchants display goods to discourage shoplifting?

Why

- Why prosecute shoplifters?
- Why document shoplifting incidents?
- Why engage in shoplifting prevention programs?
- Why spend money in shoplifting detection or prevention programs?

The following chapters address these and other important questions about shoplifting.

NOTES

1. *Knickerbocker News* (Albany, N.Y.), May 14, 1980, p. 14A.
2. *Hayes Report on Loss Prevention,* vol. 5, no. 2 (Spring 1990). Published quarterly by Jack L. Hayes International, Inc., Stanfordville, NY.
3. "A Growing Problem in Our Nation," *Peter Berlin Report on Shrinkage Control,* Executive Edition (February 1990). Published by Peter Berlin Consulting Group, Inc., Jericho, NY.
4. Personal communication, Fall 1989.
5. "New Study on Shrinkage in the United Kingdom," *Peter Berlin Report on Shrinkage Control,* Executive Edition (April 1989). Published by Peter Berlin Consulting Group, Inc., Jericho, NY.
6. "A Growing Problem in Our Nation."
7. Ibid.
8. Ibid.
9. Ibid.

2

Shoplifters

The term *shoplifting* refers to a rather specific and narrow category of larceny. It is best defined as an act of theft from a retailer committed during the hours the store is open to the public by a person who is or appears to be a legitimate customer. Hence, retail employees who steal from their employers, vendor representatives who pilfer goods while in the store to restock shelves, and crooks who hide in the restroom just before the store closes in preparation for burglarizing it later are not shoplifting. They're engaged in other types of larceny.

Shoplifters fall into two categories, although the distinction between the two sometimes becomes blurred. People who engage in shoplifting are either professionals or amateurs. Their motivation for stealing is the determinative factor that places them in one or the other category. At the risk of oversimplification, the professional's motive is income; that is, so-called professional shoplifters steal for a living. Those who steal for any other reason are normally categorized as amateurs.

Note that these two terms fail to address directly the issue of skill. There are certainly amateur shoplifters who are quite adept, or "professional," in the way they steal, and conversely there may be some professional shoplifters who, in the early stages of their careers, are "amateurish" in their work. Be that as it may, as used here the two terms focus on the *why* and not the *how*.

Before discussing the individual categories, it's important to keep in mind that there is no stereotypical shoplifter in either category. One cannot look for a person who fits a particular description; shoplifters come in different sizes, ages, and sexes, and from varying ethnic, educational, and economic backgrounds. Thus, to form a mental image of the typical shoplifter is a mistake. Shoplifters may steal while store owners who have formed a mental image of a shoplifter are oblivious to them because the owners are looking for someone who does not exist, missing, meanwhile, the actual shoplifter.

AMATEURS

Amateur shoplifters generally steal on impulse, that is, without a preconceived plan. They typically rationalize the act of theft along the following lines: It is okay to take this because

1. the store's prices are too high
2. the store makes too much profit
3. the store offers poor, insufficient, or discourteous service

As indicated earlier, the primary difference between the amateur and the professional is the motivation for the theft. Amateurs steal occasionally out of a desire to possess and use the item stolen or to give the item as a gift. More often than not, the amateur shoplifter has the means to pay for the stolen article. There are exceptions, of course. A street person may not have the money to pay for a bottle of wine; a drug addict may not have the cash to pay for a stolen radio—indeed, the addict's motive may be to convert the radio to cash to pay for drugs. Very few amateurs steal out of legitimate necessity. The proverbial mother who steals a loaf of bread to feed her starving children rarely exists.

After their first successful effort, some amateur shoplifters report getting a "high" or a "rush" from stealing, and they begin to steal repeatedly, no longer simply because the opportunity presents itself but because of the thrill involved. Amateur shoplifters who develop this "shoplifting is a thrill" syndrome can be particularly vexing to merchants because they become quite proficient at stealing, even though they are still classed as amateurs.

The thefts of the amateur shoplifter account for the largest number of shoplifting incidents but not necessarily the largest percentage of losses financially. The loss resulting from each amateur incident is small compared to the loss from each professional theft. Every type of retail establishment experiences losses caused by amateurs, but professionals tend to gravitate to the up-scale and fashion stores because of the commercial nature of their work.

Amateur shoplifters can be subclassified as follows:

- preteens
- teenagers
- mentally disturbed individuals
- adult shoplifters

Preteens

Youngsters in the primary grades do engage in shoplifting and are quite impressionable when caught. Their conduct is often discovered at home by concerned and responsible parents who bring the kids back to the store to return the item and apologize. This action often has a positive impact on these children. Store management personnel should handle this situation in a somber and expeditious manner—not making too much of it but not minimizing it either. One can't help but wonder what percentage of the children who were caught by the merchant or by the family and whose cases were improperly handled continued to steal in later years. Indeed, this could be the most overlooked opportunity to prevent future shoplifting. Strategists working to educate preteens to say no to drug use are years ahead of loss prevention practitioners in the retail community.

Teenagers

Teenage shoplifters are usually amateurs, although some develop shoplifting skills that a professional would envy. Experience has shown that at least 50% of teenage shoplifters come from affluent homes and do not steal out of necessity. Why then do so many teens shoplift? There seems to be a variety of reasons. Some teens shoplift because of peer pressure or because they've been told it's a harmless way to get things they would not otherwise have. Some teens shoplift because they see it as a way of expressing themselves—of not playing by the rules. Occasionally, a teen club requires prospective members to shoplift as an initiation rite: Both boys' and girls' clubs have been guilty of such practices. Other teenagers develop the idea that a certain amount of cheating is permissible: They hear Dad talk about how he cheated on his income taxes or Mom talks about how the salesclerk missed an item in her bag and she was not charged for it. Television and other media often give the impression that large corporations are not good citizens, or are "ripping off the public," leaving impressionable teens with the idea that it's permissible to steal from a large company.

Unfortunately, many teens and some adults shoplift as a means of getting attention or help with other problems. Parental inattention or overprotectiveness can provide the impetus for a teenager to shoplift. When advised that their child has been apprehended stealing, many parents are surprised when the child offers to return a closetful of stolen clothes or a drawerful of stolen jewelry. Why were these parents unaware of the stolen items in their home?

Mentally Disturbed Individuals

This subclassification represents the smallest threat to the retailer, but because the phenomenon of kleptomania invariably surfaces in discussions on shoplifting, it deserves attention here. People who suffer from kleptomania are mentally ill and require medical attention. They have an uncontrollable urge to steal a given item of merchandise that is personally symbolic. Kleptomaniacs are rarely encountered by merchants or security practitioners. Equally rare are those few individuals who, because of mental impairment or senility, simply don't comprehend the difference between right and wrong conduct or don't grasp the consequences of their actions. Seasoned security practitioners know that criminal prosecution is pointless, wasteful, and perhaps cruel, and that these cases must be handled in an exceptional way.

When a kleptomaniac is apprehended and the family is notified or learns of the incident, the family normally arranges to pay for the stolen items. Known klepto-maniacs can be kept under constant observation when in the store, a record kept of what they have shoplifted, and the family billed for the items on a prearranged basis. This method of handling kleptomaniacs avoids embarrassing them and their families and also protects the store from losses.

Adult Shoplifters

At the risk of creating a new line of defense for criminal lawyers or legitimatizing misconduct, we nonetheless must recognize that many adults have claimed that they took merchandise not with evil intent but rather because of some disorientation due to midlife crisis or menopause. There may be some truth to that, and there may not be. Even with years of experience and after reviewing literally tens of thousands of shoplifting arrests, it's still difficult to explain why a middle-aged, educated, profes-sional woman would steal a bottle of perfume. Some claim to be disoriented due to menopause and the medication they take for that condition. This is not to say that menopause is a legitimate excuse for shoplifting, but readers should be aware of this phenomenon. It may explain why so many middle-aged women of apparent means are involved in shoplifting. Some adult shoplifters steal hoping they will be caught and then receive medical or psychological help. Shoplifting as a means of manifesting a call for help, although rare, does occur.

PROFESSIONALS

Professional shoplifters, although significantly fewer in number than the amateurs, account for a greater financial loss per shoplifting incident. Professional shoplifters steal for profit. They rarely keep stolen merchandise for their personal use; instead they sell it on the street for a small percentage of its worth or fence it through people or organizations that specialize in buying and reselling stolen property. Profes-sional shoplifters often steal to support a drug habit.

Drug Users

Drug users who shoplift deserve the professional label; they shoplift only to obtain money, and the money is used almost exclusively to purchase drugs. Drug addicts have been known to steal huge quantities of merchandise daily to support their habits. When one considers the facts—stolen, or "boosted," merchandise is usually sold for about 10% to 20% of its retail value, and many addicts have habits of $100 or $200 a day—it's easy to calculate that drug addicts must steal from $500 to $2000 in merchandise a day to support their habits.

Some addicts attempt to return merchandise to the store where they stole it or to another store selling similar goods for a cash refund, claiming that the goods were a gift. This technique provides full cash value for the stolen goods and requires addicts to do less work to obtain their daily drug money.

When apprehended shoplifting, addicts tend to be more antagonistic and violent than amateurs, so caution must be exercised when dealing with them.

Early Accounts of Shoplifting

In his book *Security Control: External Theft,*[1] Bob Curtis notes that one of the earliest recorded accounts of professional shoplifting was written in 1597. By 1726, shoplifters had become so common that merchants asked the government for help in apprehending them. The government offered a reward and a pardon to anyone who would inform on these thieves. Another reference to shoplifting was described in *The Lives of Remarkable Criminals,* which was published in London in 1753. This publication reported the activities of three shoplifters who fenced their stolen merchandise through "thief taker" Jonathan Wilde. One of the three shoplifters informed on her two associates and their fence. As a result, the three were apprehended, tried, and executed. Shoplifting has survived essentially unchanged for over 200 years. The punishment, for better or for worse, has not survived unchanged.

Strategies Used by Professionals

Professional shoplifters target trendy, best-selling, or high-value merchandise for which they can obtain a good price on the street or through a fence. Professionals rarely work alone, but rather coordinate in teams of two or more. Some members of the team act as decoys, occupying sales help while other members of the gang do the stealing. Most professionals research store layouts and quick avenues of escape, and if security personnel are employed, they quickly learn their identities. Some of the most successful professionals are well dressed and businesslike in appearance; they look just like the customers most retailers try to attract.

Professionals may employ means other than the ones traditionally ascribed to shoplifters. Female professionals are expert at "working" fitting rooms and can often easily confuse the fitting room attendant or by-pass normal fitting room controls. Professionals who specialize in jewelry frequently steal by distracting sales associates or by palm-and-switch methods—a technique in which the merchandise is palmed and cheap look-alike goods are switched. This is accomplished while the salesperson is momentarily distracted, often by an accomplice.

Another method used by professionals is selecting and gathering up merchandise to be stolen, putting it in a shopping bag, or simply bunching it together and secreting or hiding it somewhere on the selling floor—usually under a fixture or a rack full of merchandise. After the goods are set up, an accomplice enters the store and removes the merchandise while the original shoplifter distracts the salesperson.

Other professionals "case," or reconnoiter, the store to identify vulnerable merchandise, such as expensive and desirable goods placed near entrances or exits. These goods are vulnerable to grab-and-run thefts, which are used by many of the less sophisticated professionals and drug addicts.

Foreign Gangs

Recent years have seen the proliferation of professional shoplifters who enter the United States, rent cars, and travel wide areas of the country (for example, the entire West Coast from San Diego to Seattle). They steal merchandise and ship it back to their native land, where it fetches more money than it would if fenced in the U.S. A group known as *The Columbians* has been active at this activity for several years, and few members have been apprehended.

These gangs are compartmentalized with little or no organizational contact. If one member is apprehended, he or she has little information to offer about the gang or its leadership and hence is of little value to the authorities in their efforts to counter this activity. The gangs are highly skilled at shoplifting, extremely mobile, and well financed. They are a formidable threat to retailers across the United States. When members of professional shoplifting gangs are apprehended, it is not uncommon to learn that merchandise worth tens of thousands of dollars had been stolen in a matter of a few days.

SUMMARY

Retailers, their agents, and employees must recognize that there is no such thing as a stereotypical shoplifter; they come in all sizes, shapes, ages, and backgrounds; they steal for a variety of reasons, and their presence is inconspicuous and constant. Shoplifters are broadly divided into those whose income is derived from the thefts— the professionals—and those who steal for any other reason—the amateurs. Amateurs are more prevalent, but professionals cause a substantially greater financial loss per incident of theft. Drug users who steal to support their habit fall into the professional category because they convert stolen goods into cash for the immediate purchase of drugs. Some have habits that amount to $2000 worth of retail merchandise per day.

NOTE

1. Bob Curtis, *Security Control: External Theft* (New York: Chain Store Publishing Corporation, a subsidiary of Lebhar-Friedman, Inc., 1978).

3

The Mechanics of Shoplifting

Shoplifting can be accomplished through any one of a variety of known and predictable strategies, which may be referred to as the *mechanics of shoplifting*. These known and predictable strategies are

- walking out with goods exposed
- walking out with goods concealed
- grab-and-run theft
- "crotching"
- booster equipment
- ticket switching
- grazing
- fraudulent returns
- diversion
- collusion

The phrase *known and predictable strategies* might suggest there may be some *unknown* methods of shoplifting, but that's not the case. The mechanics of shoplifting will invariably fall under one or more of the strategies just listed. Shoplifters may employ some creative nuances to disguise the act, such as handing an item of merchandise to a small child who carries the item from the store. When the parent and child are stopped, the parent feigns surprise and anger at the child (the child is truly innocent and an unwitting party to the crime). Once the strategies are understood, the subtle (and not too subtle) variations become apparent.

WALKING OUT WITH GOODS EXPOSED

Walking out of the store with merchandise that has not been purchased, whether it is openly carried or worn, is a relatively unsophisticated method of theft. Shoplifters who use this method wait until no one is looking, select an item of merchandise, and depending on the item and its size, either put it on or simply walk out the door with it as though it were their own.

One caution should be mentioned in connection with observing this type of shoplifting. Some customers return to the store with a legitimately purchased item and, because they don't want to wait for a sales clerk, effect their own exchange. These unofficial exchange procedures can be misleading; it would be easy for the merchant to make an honest but costly mistake in falsely accusing a customer of theft. Before stopping customers for shoplifting, even after observing them openly pick up merchandise and walk out with it, it is vital that you ensure that they did not arrive with a similar item.

WALKING OUT WITH GOODS CONCEALED

Most merchandise that is shoplifted leaves the store concealed in some fashion.

Use of Clothing

Many shoplifters select an item to steal, and when the opportunity presents itself (that is, when they feel they are not being observed by anyone), they secrete the item under their clothes or in a pocket and then leave the store. This technique is especially adaptable to the theft of expensive silk dresses, which can be balled up into the size of a tennis ball and easily concealed. Before Roger Griffin's retirement in 1990, his annual shoplifting report addressed the supermarket, drug, and discount store segment of the retail industry. In 1985 he reported that approximately 60% of all items were removed from stores either in a pocket or under the thief's clothing. [1]

For years new sales associates were cautioned to watch for people who wear raincoats on sunny days; they were suspected of wearing the raincoat to conceal stolen merchandise. Although our experience has shown that today's shoplifters are more sophisticated and that this caution is probably more proverbial than useful, the "baggy coat" technique is still encountered and is a favorite of shoplifters who specialize in the theft of fur coats, bulky leather clothing, and hard goods such as housewares, cigarettes, liquor, and packaged meats.

Shopping Bags

Shopping bags are particularly dangerous in terms of their potential use as a vehicle for removing stolen merchandise, especially for department stores and stores that do not have a front-end check-out configuration. The popularity of shopping bags among shoplifters and their inherent danger to the retailer lie in the rather universal assumption that goods already in a bag have been purchased. This assumption is particularly common when customers walk around in one store carrying a bag from another store. Regrettably, merchants are often the unwitting accomplices of thieves when they provide on request a shopping bag to a "customer" who has made no purchase and has no apparent need for it. In most cases, however, shoplifters bring their own bags into the store, either carrying them and making them appear to contain purchases or folding them up and concealing them from view.

A popular technique used by shoplifters involves placing a shopping bag on the floor under a rounder or other merchandise display fixture. The shoplifter drops merchandise from the fixture into the shopping bag. When the bag is full, the thief simply picks up the bag and leaves the area. While dropping the merchandise into the bag, the shoplifter makes every attempt to appear to be a legitimate customer. In fact, removing merchandise from the rack and "examining" it before replacing it in a manner that allows it to fall into the shopping bag is part of the strategy.

Other Hand-Carries

Merchandise can be secreted in a variety of hand-carried items other than shopping bags. For example, ladies' handbags are used in 25% to 28% of all shoplifting incidents, according to Griffin's 1985 report.[2] Small items can be dropped into closed umbrellas; flat items, such as discs and records, can be placed between book pages; articles can be deposited in bookbags, attaché cases, and virtually any item that has a capacity to conceal the desired article. If only diaper bags and baby strollers could talk!

Fitting Rooms

Many of the specific techniques of shoplifting can be used in a fitting room. Fitting rooms are a very popular place for shoplifters to do their stealing because they shield shoplifters from casual observation and provide them with a feeling of security that their criminal activity will go unobserved. Specific fitting room control techniques designed to minimize exposure to shoplifting are discussed in detail in Chapter 7.

GRAB-AND-RUN THEFT

The grab-and-run technique is the most unsophisticated, brazen, and thuglike shoplifting technique that will be encountered. The most vulnerable store areas are those near entrances and exits, particularly those with streets or roadways immediately outside. The grab-and-run technique is simple: The thief simply grabs an armload of merchandise from a display and runs out the nearest exit, more than likely to a waiting car driven by an accomplice.

"CROTCHING"

Retailers and security practitioners hear numerous apocryphal stories about shop-lifters who have stolen 12-pound frozen turkeys, typewriters, or cases of beer by walking out of the store with the item hidden between their legs by a large, flowing skirt. Many of these recitals are the result of one incident that is repeated many times. However, the ability of some professional shoplifters to "crotch" merchandise is well developed; we have personally witnessed shoplifters who were able to hold a large variety of goods between their legs, including a full-length mink coat, and still walk in a normal fashion. This technique is certainly used by professionals although it is infrequently encountered. A so-called shoplifters' school in Los Angeles trained women in this technique by having them practice with telephone directories. When they could master holding these heavy and slippery books between their thighs while walking with an inconspicuous gait, that portion of their training was successfully completed.

BOOSTER EQUIPMENT

Booster is a slang word for shoplifter, and *to boost* is synonymous with *to lift*. Other definitions of *boost* include to aid or assist. Hence, booster equipment is any form of paraphernalia that can be used to aid or assist a shoplifter in the act of theft. Booster equipment includes such items as booster boxes, bloomers, girdles, cages, coats, and purses.

The typical booster box is a cardboard box that is large enough to conceal the items to be stolen and that is wrapped in either brown wrapping paper or, at Christmas time, gift wrapping, and then securely tied with twine or string. The objective is to give the appearance of a securely wrapped package. The booster box is fabricated so that one side of the package opens and is held in place by a spring. While carrying the booster box, the shoplifter can feed stolen items into the box through the trap door. The trap door closes after the stolen items are inserted, giving the appearance of a normally wrapped package. In some cases, shoplifters set the box down over an item, and the spring door allows the item to be admitted to the box. They slide the box carefully from the display table, manipulating the box and the concealed item to permit the hinged side to close, and casually carry the box from the store.

Booster bloomers, which are reminiscent of nineteenth-century ladies' under-wear, have a flexible elastic waistband, and the legs are tied off just above the knee. The billowy legs accommodate items that are dropped down or shoved down from the waist and are effectively concealed under the outer skirt.

Booster girdles work in much the same fashion. The shoplifter wears a large, stretchable girdle or undergarment that is capable of receiving and holding stolen merchandise. She surreptitiously places it there by pulling out the waistband of her skirt. Women who use booster girdles try to appear heavier than they are when they enter the store so that after the booster girdle has been loaded with stolen merchandise their appearance remains the same.

Booster cages are hollow cages designed to make a woman appear to be pregnant. They're often fabricated out of wire, and the straps that hold them (and the stolen articles contained therein) go around the body.

Booster coats are loosely fitting top coats. They are similar to trench coats, but the inner lining has been reconstructed to form large pockets. An item placed into the bottomless pocket drops down into the lining. Another version of the booster coat has exposed hooks sewn onto the inside of the coat. The hooks hold soft goods that are quickly stuffed through the coat's front opening. The shoplifter simply opens the coat with one hand and with the other "hangs" an item inside on a sharp hook.

The booster purse is a ladies' handbag with a bottom that has been modified to open. The purse can be set on a counter containing merchandise, such as a cosmetics counter, and while appearing to be digging about for her wallet, the thief reaches through the purse's contents and through the opening, seizes the desired item, pulls the item back up into the purse, releases the stolen item, and withdraws her hand. It's virtually impossible to see the theft, especially if the purse is set down on the item to be taken.

Boosting equipment is used mostly by professional shoplifters. In many jurisdictions, a shoplifter who uses a booster is considered to be in possession of burglar tools, which raises shoplifting from a misdemeanor to a felony. Because the possession of booster devices increases the seriousness of the crime considerably and their mere possession is often prima-facie evidence of intent to commit a felony, most amateurs and even many professionals avoid taking this risk.

TICKET SWITCHING

In some jurisdictions, ticket switching is not legally considered shoplifting, but it is certainly a method whereby a thief can obtain merchandise without paying the full price for it. In ticket switching, the customer removes the price ticket from an inexpensive item, affixes the ticket to an expensive but similar piece of merchandise, and then pays the lower price. A popular place for switching tickets is in fitting rooms, although bolder ticket switchers do it on the selling floor.

A caution when dealing with ticket switchers: The possibility always exists that the lower-priced ticket was mistakenly placed on the item by a careless store employee. Thus when dealing with ticket switchers, it is important that you observe the actual switch and are able to recover the original ticket from where the culprit stashed it.

A variation of the ticket switch is the container switch. For example, athletic shoes are displayed in boxes that have various prices, depending on the quality and style of shoe. The shoplifter switches shoes and presents to the cashier the box that bears a price tag of $59.99 and contains shoes that sell for $79.99—an attempted theft of $20. A creative thief can switch four sticks of butter with four sticks of margarine and present the cashier with a margarine box containing butter.

GRAZING

Grazing refers to customers who consume food items before paying for them, for example, a customer bags one and a half pounds of grapes in the produce department, eats some as she continues her shopping, and by the time she pays for her groceries at the checkstand she has only one pound left.

FRAUDULENT RETURNS

Refunding merchandise is a natural and anticipated part of the retailing process. Customers have a myriad of legitimate reasons to return goods: The item may be defective, spoiled, broken, or the wrong size; or perhaps it has shrunk or faded or it's a duplicate gift.

Fraudulent returns are masked efforts to convert stolen goods into their full retail value in cash or credit on one's account. Thieves use a common reason to justify or explain the return. The refunding act is either an interrupted and disconnected part of the original act of shoplifting (or employee theft) or a direct and uninterrupted part of the act of theft. An example of the former: A shoplifter steals the article in one store on Monday and returns it to another store for cash on Tuesday. An example of the latter: A thief selects an item from a counter at 2:30 on Monday, puts the item in a store bag, and presents the item to the cashier at 2:40 for a refund, never even leaving the store. If the refund act is not a direct and uninterrupted part of the act of theft, it is usually impossible to prove that the refund is fraudulent (and a crime). Perhaps that's why fraudulent refunding flourishes. Once shoplifters get away with the goods, it's theirs.

Shoplifters who sell stolen merchandise on the street or to a fence are lucky to receive 25% of its retail value. By returning the stolen item to the store from which it was taken and exchanging it for cash, shoplifters are able to get full value for the stolen item. Current law requires that merchants pay in cash charge account credit balances when requested to do so by the customer. This law permits shoplifters to return stolen goods as a "credit to account" and then ask the merchant to pay the credit balance in cash. Credit balances can be used to purchase gift certificates, which can also be converted to cash, either by direct conversion to cash (if the merchant permits this questionable practice) or by purchasing an inexpensive item, paying with the gift certificate, and receiving cash as change. With the recent increase in drug use, which has created a never-ending requirement for large sums of cash, fraudulent returns are an increasingly popular method among addicts. They shoplift and then return the stolen goods, claiming it was a gift for which they have no receipt.

Interestingly, not all fraudulent refunds are conducted by shoplifters and dishonest employees. We have experienced situations where goods are salvaged, wholesaled, or sold at cost by retailers, wholesalers, shippers, and even manufacturers because of some type of damage. These goods end up in outlet stores that sell distressed merchandise at low prices. Typically, the manufacturer's label and retailer's tickets are supposed to be removed, but they sometimes aren't. Subsequently, greedy people who see the potential for a good return on investment purchase the distressed goods and return them to unwitting retailers for full value.

It is not uncommon for shoplifters to purchase an article just for the receipt and steal a like item to facilitate a return. Similarly, some shoplifters pick up receipts and steal the item or items listed as part of a theft defense or refund strategy.

DIVERSION TECHNIQUES

A technique that can be employed in conjunction with any of the shoplifting methods previously described is diversion. An accomplice or accomplices of the shoplifter employs various methods to distract the store employee so that the shoplifter can operate without interference and with little likelihood of discovery. Techniques used to distract sales associates range from simply seeking help in selecting merchandise outside the shoplifter's target area to staging loud and disturbing arguments or fights and even feigning illness. Should such events occur, employees must be alert to the possibility that attention is being diverted from criminal activity.

COLLUSION

Some shoplifters operate in cooperation with accomplices who are store employees. Occasionally—and particularly during big sale events or during the Christmas season—individuals apply for work with the sole intention of assisting others in shoplifting from the premises while they are on duty. The loot from collusive thefts is usually split between the actual shoplifter and the employee-accomplice. Employees may simply turn their head at the theft or passively assist their accomplices by alerting them to the presence of security personnel or other employees. Other employee-accomplices may actively assist in the theft by setting up merchandise to be stolen and then alerting their accomplices to its location. When collusive activity between an employee and an outside shoplifter can be proven, most jurisdictions consider both parties equally guilty of the theft.

Collusion could also include a situation involving two or more nonemployees in which the shoplifter takes the merchandise from its display and surreptitiously passes the stolen item to an accomplice, who carries it out of the store. As an illustration, picture this: Three teenagers remove a crystal vase from its display and then enter an elevator going down. They walk, turn, and stand close together. An older woman carrying a shopping bag also enters the elevator. The store security agent, maintaining a continuous surveillance, also enters the elevator cab. The teenagers crowd together facing the front of the elevator in front of the older woman (who is their confederate) and drop the vase into her shopping bag. If the agent stops the youths, they will not have the vase. If the agent finds the vase in the woman's bag, she will claim she was victimized and is innocent.

SUMMARY

People who shoplift use a wide array of strategies to remove merchandise from a retailer, such as carrying goods out as though they owned it, concealing goods in a variety of containers or on their person, grabbing and running with goods, concealing goods between their legs, using booster equipment, switching price tickets or merchandise containers, consuming food before paying for it, claiming fraudulent refunds, and various acts of diversion and collusion.

The retailer's defense consists of an informed and knowledgeable staff that understands not only the methodology of shoplifting but also how to prevent theft. If the retailer has the luxury of professional security practitioners on staff, their coordination and cooperation with informed sales and nonselling employees will go a long way in detecting shoplifting and in reducing losses.

NOTES

1. Roger Griffin, *Commercial Service Systems' 22nd Annual Report on Shoplifting in Supermarkets, Drug Stores, and Discount Stores,* Los Angeles, 1985.
2. Ibid.

4

Selecting Security Personnel

It's a universally accepted axiom that the strength or weakness of any organization lies in the quality of its personnel. The nature of an employee's job responsibilities dictates the level of quality required. The greater the responsibilities, the greater the investment required in the employee selection process. Hence, less effort is expended in selecting a janitor than in selecting a cashier or a security employee.

The proper selection of retail security employees is extremely important. The actions of all employees when dealing with a suspected shoplifter must be reasonable and conform to various legal requirements, but the way in which security people handle these situations is judged much more critically. Security people are employees whose primary responsibility is handling security matters; employment presupposes that these people have been properly selected and trained and that they will perform their duties in accordance with established standards.

When dealing with shoplifters, sales clerks, store owners, and security people must understand that the situation is by nature confrontational. The suspected shoplifter will be detained, however briefly, and this detention has implications for the individual's fundamental civil rights. The Bill of Rights guarantees everyone freedom from deprivation of life, liberty, or property without due process of law and protection against unreasonable searches and seizures. Federal and state laws make violations of these fundamental rights either a crime or a tort (a civil wrong that can be redressed in the courts) to which severe penalties are attached. Thus, should a suspected shoplifter be dealt with in a manner that violates these rights, both the individual who commits the violation and the employer may be subject to severe penalties.

The standard of care to which a business or its employees will be held is generally one of reasonableness; the standard to which a security person is held is generally much higher than that to which a sales employee is held, on the assumption that a security person is a specialist and is expected to have more expertise in dealing with security matters than other employers. It is therefore important that all employees who must deal with the shoplifting problem be given some degree of training in how to interact with shoplifters, but it is *essential* that security personnel be thoroughly trained in this subject.

Before security personnel can be trained, they must be hired. Should security people be employees of the business just like sales associates and stock clerks, or should they be contract security employees, that is, hired from a guard or outside security services company? The issue of proprietary versus contract security is a topic unto itself, but whichever decision is made, the same general issues of selection and training exist. In the case of contract personnel, though, the job falls to the security firm rather than the retail business owner. This does not relieve the retail business owner of all responsibility, however, because any civil lawsuit brought by a shoplifter will invariably name the retail business as a defendant. Therefore, when using contract security personnel, merchants must ensure that proper selection and training were used by the security services firm they have engaged. This precaution will provide that some minimum level of civil liability protection is ensured.

NEGLIGENT HIRING

Why is the proper selection of security personnel so important, and how can a business owner be sure it is done properly? Security personnel selection has taken on more importance since the mid-1980s, when the United States experienced an increase in civil suits against employers for the tort of negligent hiring. This cause of action was almost unknown previously, but it has developed into a major cause of action in recent years. A tort of negligent hiring normally arises after an employee allegedly commits a wrong against a customer (legally known as a *business invitee)*. Negligent hiring means essentially that an employer was negligent in hiring a particular person (the employee who "injured" the customer) and that the employer knew— *or should have known*—that there was a likelihood (the legal term is *forseeability)* that this employee would engage in this injurious (tortious) behavior. How should the employer have foreseen this? By adequately looking into the background of the potential employee before hiring. Considering the adversarial and confrontational aspects of a security person's job and the very real potential for adverse judgments and resulting financial damages against businesses for negligent hiring, it is apparent that the proper selection of security personnel is extremely important.

The importance of loss prevention personnel selection was the topic of an article in a national security publication, portions of which may clarify this issue.[1]

> In order to understand how . . . negligent hiring . . . evolved, it is useful to review a bit of history. Employers have always been responsible for negligent acts of their employees, under the traditional principal/agent doctrine known as *"respondeat superior."* It was only if the employee could be shown to have acted outside the scope of his employment duties that the employer could escape liability for unreasonable

or excessive conduct. In the case of . . . security personnel . . . this risk is perhaps at its greatest. The normal requirements of these jobs often entail certain actions that might be deemed unreasonable, if committed by other individuals in other settings.

The concept of negligent hiring [was] developed to close off the last major avenue of escape for employer liability. Under these related theories, an employer can be held liable even for acts which are clearly outside the scope of an employee's normal duties, if the employer either knew, or should have been able to determine, that the employee had a propensity to commit such misconduct.

"Negligent hiring" has been defined as a breach of the employer's duty to make adequate investigation of an employee's fitness before hiring. While claims of negligent hiring can be lodged against almost any type of employee who acts outside the scope of his employment, it would seem that loss prevention personnel are prime targets for this kind of case [and] there seems to be a higher standard imposed upon loss prevention personnel to act reasonably in all situations.

The negligent hiring of security employees, whether contract or proprietary, is an important topic. Two other references that discuss this subject in some detail are worth reading: *Labor and Unemployment Law Update* of March 27, 1989,[2] and "Understanding the Liability of Negligent Hiring" by Norman D. Bates, J.D.[3]

REGULATION OF PRIVATE SECURITY

The rather unique duties of security personnel and their increasing numbers and functions within the U.S. business community drew the attention of the federal government in the early 1970s. A major study by the Rand Corporation, *Private Police in the United States: Findings and Recommendations,* done at the request of the Department of Justice, was critical of the lack of professional standards within the private security industry. Private security had for many years been the subject of some degree of state regulation; in 1975, forty states had some type of licensing provisions covering private investigative, security guard, burglar alarm, or central station alarm companies,[4] but no states regulated proprietary security personnel. Regulated or not, only a handful of states proscribed or mandated training requirements for security personnel.

In 1976, two events occurred that had, and continue to have, a major impact on the selection and training of private contract and proprietary security personnel. These events were the publication of *Private Security,* a report by the Task Force on Private Security of the National Advisory Committee on Criminal Justice Standards and Goals[5] and the issuance of regulations by the Law Enforcement Assistance Administration (LEAA) of the U.S. Department of Justice governing the dissemination of criminal record and criminal history information.[6] The *Private Security* report was critical of existing standards and made numerous recommendations regarding selection and training requirements for private security personnel. The LEAA regulations for all intents and purposes closed criminal history records to private employers, thereby preventing the employers of private security personnel from investigating the prior criminal history of job applicants. Criminal conviction information continued to be legally obtainable, but as a practical matter its acquisition became increasingly difficult.

In 1978, the passage of the Financial Privacy Act and the subsequent passage of the Fair Credit Reporting Act also increased the difficulty of obtaining background information pertinent to security applicants. Further, the plethora of civil litigation and laws in the 1980s concerning individual privacy rights has made the investigation of former employment records nearly a meaningless exercise because to protect themselves from potential civil litigation, most companies will only disclose dates of former employment, if they disclose anything at all.

Thus, while the developments in civil law demand that we properly investigate and screen employees, particularly security employees, other areas of the law have limited and made difficult the employer's ability to adequately screen applicants. How will this dilemma be resolved, and how can employers' interests be protected?

CONTRACT SECURITY PERSONNEL

The focus of this chapter is on the selection of in-house, or proprietary, personnel, but a word is in order regarding the use of contract services. When merchants use contract personnel, in addition to obtaining and verifying references from the security services company, they should also clearly describe their expectations, restrictions, and job requirements for which they are contracting services. They should ensure that the security services company has adequate liability insurance (a minimum of $1,000,000) with a reputable carrier, and that the merchant is named as an additional insured on the service company's policy. Merchants should have a written contract with the security services company that includes any requirements particular to their business and specifies any restrictions on the duties or responsibilities of the contract security personnel. For example, a contract may set forth the specific circumstances under which a customer may be approached about shoplifting and the manner in which the confrontation is to be handled, including the language to be used. The degree and method of supervision of contract personnel is also extremely important and should be made part of the contract. Competent legal advice is highly recommended in establishing these requirements and incorporating them into the security services contract. The use of a contract security service is not a shield against civil liability for the improper or injurious actions of contract personnel.[7]

PROPRIETARY SECURITY PERSONNEL

How should proprietary security personnel be selected, and what procedures can merchants follow to obtain a quality security person and minimize litigation for negligent hiring? Many areas pertinent to a security applicant's background are the same as those of any other applicant, but several areas take on significantly greater importance. The following background elements must be scrutinized more carefully for security candidates.

Appearance

The appearance of a loss prevention person is important for several reasons. The confrontational and adversarial nature of the security agent's contact with the public has been discussed. The agent's appearance must demand respect yet not appear threatening to customers. A neat and well-groomed appearance and a soft-spoken but authoritative bearing can help to avoid conflicts and situations that may escalate out of control. These are attributes of security professionals. Obviously, those who are or appear to be incapable of taking physical and psychological control of a situation are at a distinct disadvantage, and they are probably not the ones to select for a security position.

Education

The job of a security or loss prevention agent (the term *security guard* more appropriately applies to a uniformed person who patrols or guards physical property or controls ingress and egress from a defined area) certainly does not require the mental acuity of a surgeon. Conversely, the verbal and written communication skills needed to adequately handle a security job, suggest that the candidate have at least a high school education. Junior or community college courses or a bachelor's degree are certainly an advantage. When looking at a candidate's education, consider writing skills in particular because nearly every activity of a loss prevention agent eventually becomes the subject of a written report. Verbal communication skills are also extremely important. In their contact with the public, security people reflect you and your business. Their ability to communicate effectively and politely is essential from a public relations point of view, and it is equally important in presenting the facts regarding an encounter with a suspected shoplifter to the authorities. These same skills are put to use when security agents must testify in court.

Character

Of all of the attributes or qualifications that are desirable for security personnel to possess, character (which includes attitudes, morals, and values) is the most important. Character is generally fully formulated by the time a person completes high school, and there's little chance that one's character can be reshaped by business or industry, though there are always exceptions.

The following characteristics should disqualify applicants for security positions:

- candidates who carry a grudge
- candidates who are racially or religiously biased
- candidates who have an overbearing personality
- candidates who are prone to violence
- candidates who lack objectivity
- candidates who are deceitful or dishonest
- candidates who lack a sense of humor
- candidates who are overly rigid, sensitive, or suspicious
- candidates who lack ethics

The selection process is aimed at uncovering these character flaws.

Writing Skills

One of the first things an apprentice security agent learns is that just about everything that occurs in connection with the job will become the subject of a written report. These reports must be factual, accurate, and concise, and they must be able to convey to others a clear picture of the events. The written report is often the only means by which the security agent and the employer are judged by those reviewing the incident. Police agencies, prosecuting attorneys, defense attorneys, insurance carriers, and occasionally the press will all judge the professionalism of the security staff by the quality of the written report prepared about an incident or apprehension.

How can you ascertain the level of an applicant's writing skills? Writing tests (having the applicant write a sample report or narrative) may or may not be legal; the test's construction, application, and relevance, as well as how it is scored, will determine if the test is discriminatory—and illegal—or permissible. What are alternatives to such tests? One technique that must be consistently applied to all applicants, is to ask each applicant to list prior employment (or, if no prior employment, courses taken in high school) and to write a paragraph about each job or course, describing the good and bad aspects of each. The applicant might also be asked to simply write a resume and describe the duties and responsibilities of each position. This technique also provides an example of the applicant's handwriting. Is it legible? Is the spelling correct? As imperfect as these methods are, they do provide information that might not be obtained any other way. Before using any employment screening technique, it is advisable to check with an attorney to ensure that you do not violate any federal, state, or local antidiscrimination or other applicable laws.

Observation Skills

Security or loss prevention employees must have the required concentration to see everything a potential shoplifter does and must recall with clarity and in detail what they have seen at a later time when it can be put into a written report. Security

agents must observe and remember details that may be crucial to establishing sufficient evidence to support an arrest and prosecution.

Admittedly, it is difficult to test an applicant for observation skills. Again, there
are legal considerations. It may be permissible to place a unique object on your desk
during the interview with the applicant. After the interview is over, outside the
office, you might casually ask the applicant a question about the object to determine
whether or not he or she saw it, remembers it in any detail, and can discuss it with
some degree of specificity. You might also inquire about a place with which both
you and the applicant are acquainted—perhaps a distant city, a local tourist attraction,
or something along these lines. Again, the caveat about legal advice is relevant.

Career Objectives

It is unreasonable and impractical to expect that every security applicant will want
to make security a life-long career. Many, if not most, people entering the private
security field at an entry-level position are accepting employment only as a temporary
job. In 1972, the Rand report[8] was highly critical of the caliber of private security
personnel. The *Private Security* report indicated that over 40% of private security
personnel accepted the position "because they were unemployed and this was the
best job they could find."[9]

The security profession has progressed significantly since 1972, primarily through
the efforts of the American Society for Industrial Security (ASIS) and its Certified
Protection Professional (CPP) program and the International Foundation for Protection Officers and its Certified Protection Officer (CPO) program. Additionally,
various other industry trade associations, such as the National Retail Federation
(formerly the National Retail Merchants Association) and its Security Board Advisory
Group, began recognizing the importance of the security function within business
and started holding annual security seminars for members. Finally, numerous colleges
and universities instituted degree programs emphasizing security as a specialty under
the administration of justice curriculum. As a result of these efforts, the security
discipline is recognized by most companies today as a vital contributor to the prof-
itability and well-being of the business, just like other more traditional functions.
Today, most of the heads of security at major corporations and businesses are vice
presidents, testifying to the recognition of the professionalism that the security
discipline has achieved over the last 20 years.

All of this progress notwithstanding, it is still true that too many entry-level
security personnel enter the field with no intention of making it a career. Unfortunately, many use the private security position as a steppingstone to another career
or as a temporary position; some have the long-range goal of entering public law
enforcement. However admirable their goal, these applicants accept and occupy
positions that more career-minded applicants might have filled. Their relatively short
tenure also creates a higher turnover rate than desirable, which is both disruptive
and costly. Fortunately, increasing numbers of applicants, many with either associate
or bachelor's degrees in security or criminal justice, see the opportunities and chal-

lenges in private security, and they make the decision to work their way up the organizational ladder within a security organization. We know more than a few people who, after rising within the security ranks, moved into other functional areas and became chief executive officers and senior vice presidents of operations for their companies. These achievements certainly speak well of the caliber of today's security executives.

Beware of applicants who exhibit the characteristics that are typical of "wannabes." A wannabe is a person who wants to be a police officer but is not qualified. These applicants know they are not qualified for public law enforcement, but they won't admit it to you or to themselves. They seek a job in private security because it is closely related to public law enforcement; they can perform some of the same functions, work closely with police officers, and think of themselves as cops. These applicants should be avoided at all costs. They are unqualified for public law enforcement for a reason, and this reason should also make them unacceptable for private security. In fairness, there is one legitimate exception to this rule: applicants who are properly motivated and who would be fully acceptable to public law enforcement except for a minor physical disability that does not disqualify them for private security employment.

Health

The job of a security agent is physically demanding. Loss prevention and security personnel must be on their feet for long periods of time; in some security positions, they must be able to crawl through ceilings and other confined areas to observe suspects or to install security surveillance equipment. Whenever a security agent arrests a shoplifter, there is always the potential for a scuffle and physical injury. The necessity of making clear observations requires good eyesight; good hearing is also important. For these reasons, applicants with back problems, bad knees, old sports injuries, and a myriad of other physical ailments or limitations should be carefully scrutinized and given a physical examination before being hired. The examining physician should be advised of the demands of the job so that he or she can make a valid recommendation as to whether the applicant's physical limitations will adversely affect his or her ability to do the job.[10]

We must keep in mind the role of security and loss prevention: to protect the assets of the company and make the company environment as safe as possible. We fail in this mission if we hire a security agent with a known physical disability that is aggravated by the demands of the job and results in a workers' compensation claim. Such situations not only deplete company assets but also increase turnover and involve the significant expense of repeating the applicant recruiting, selection, and training process for replacement personnel. Notwithstanding, compliance with the 1990 federal legislation that prohibits discriminating against the disabled must be ensured; employers must be able to clearly demonstrate that the physical limitation is specifically related to and disqualifies the candidate for the security position. For example, some disabilities may disqualify a candidate for a position as a retail security agent who makes shoplifting arrests but not for a position as a fraud investigator whose duties are primarily investigative and performed at a desk.

SELECTION TOOLS

Now that we have explored some of the attributes and skills that security employees should possess, we must examine the means by which employers can ascertain whether an applicant possesses those characteristics. Because the adequate probing of an applicant's background is a good way to minimize the potential for negligent hiring litigation and liability, this is the subject we now explore. We urge you to consult competent legal counsel before using any of these techniques to ensure that their use does not violate any statutes and that their use conforms with all current applicable laws.

Employment Application

The starting place for checking a job applicant's qualifications is the employment application, which should be required even if the applicant has provided a resume. The employment application should always require the applicant to list this minimum information:

- date of application
- applicant's full name and any other names under which he or she worked or attended school
- permanent address
- temporary mailing address (if new to area or planning to move)
- home phone number
- social security number[11]
- position desired
- schedule desired
- certification of the legal right to work in the U.S.
- details, dates, and explanation of any conviction of a crime by civilian or military court[12]
- current employment
- previous employment by this company, if any
- name of any relative employed by the company
- names of organizations to which the applicant belongs (excluding any that indicate race, sex, marital status, ancestry, national origin, or religion)
- previous employment for the past ten years, including the company, address,

job title, name of supervisor, starting and ending salary, reason for leaving, and dates of employment for each position, and periods of unemployment

- education—high school, college, and other—including name and address of the school, the course of study, dates of attendance, number of years completed, and degree earned
- military history, including dates of service, branch of service, rank at discharge, serial number, reserve status, special training, and type of discharge
- physical handicaps that would prevent the applicant from doing the job for which he or she is applying[13]
- name of person who should be notified in an emergency, with address and phone number

An employment application should also contain two additional statements regarding the veracity of the applicant's responses. The first statement should follow a notice that says, "IMPORTANT—READ AND SIGN," and it should be worded along these lines:

> The information set forth in this application is true and correct. I understand that if employed, any false or misleading statements, omissions, or failure to fully answer any question will result in my immediate dismissal, regardless of when such information is discovered. I further understand and agree that I may be bonded if employed. I agree to submit myself at any time upon request for medical examination and/or testing, as permitted by law. I authorize [company name] to secure a consumer report from consumer reporting agencies (i.e., Credit Bureau, Inc.) and to conduct such other investigation as required to verify employment in connection with my application for employment and subsequently as [company name] deems appropriate. Upon written request from me to [company name] I will be informed of the name and address of each consumer reporting agency, if any, from which a consumer report relating to me was obtained.

A second statement, in bold type opposite the place for the applicant's signature, should read, "I certify that I have read the above, understand it, and agree to it."

A careful review of the employment application can disclose various warning signs that may disqualify an applicant (such as a serious criminal conviction) or signal areas that need further investigation. For example, be wary of applicants who have unexplained periods of unemployment, who have changed jobs for a lesser salary, or who cite a "personality conflict" as the reason for leaving a job.

The strategy we recommend is, "Every question must be answered, and every answer questioned." Another recommended strategy is to note, right on the application itself, the date, time, and name of the person who confirmed former employment as well as the initials of the interviewer. This is credible proof that the company verified or at least attempted to verify the applicant's claim of former employment. After the interview, the interviewer must sign and date the application. See Figure 4–1 for a sample employment application.

EMPLOYMENT APPLICATION

IS AN EQUAL OPPORTUNITY EMPLOYER.

Please Print Clearly And Complete Both Sides Of This Employment Application. Applications Will Remain Active For One Month. Following An Offer Of Employment All Applicants Will Be Required To Supply The Following:

TODAY'S DATE

A - WORKING PAPERS (as nec.) B - SOCIAL SECURITY CARD C - PROOF OF CITIZENSHIP OR AUTHORIZATION TO WORK IN U.S.
D - NAME AND ADDRESS OF 3 REFERENCES E - PROOF OF AGE F - PERMISSION TO DO A REFERENCE AND CREDIT CHECK.

NAME (LAST) (FIRST) (MIDDLE)

HAVE YOU EVER WORKED OR ATTENDED SCHOOL UNDER ANOTHER NAME THAT WE NEED TO KNOW TO VERIFY OUR RECORDS? IF YES, NAME:
☐ YES ☐ NO

ADDRESS (NUMBER, STREET, CITY, STATE & ZIP CODE) ☐ PERMANENT ☐ TEMPORARY ☐ MAILING ADDRESS

HOME PHONE NUMBER ( ) BUSINESS OR TEMPORARY PHONE ( ) SOCIAL SECURITY NUMBER

DO YOU HAVE THE LEGAL RIGHT TO REMAIN AND WORK IN THE U.S.?
☐ YES ☐ NO

PREVIOUS RESIDENCE

CURRENTLY EMPLOYED:
☐ FULL TIME ☐ PART TIME ☐ NOT EMPLOYED

HAVE YOU EVER BEEN CONVICTED OF A CRIME (MISDEMEANORS OR FELONIES) BY A CIVILIAN OR MILITARY COURT?
☐ YES ☐ NO
Conviction Of A Crime Will Not Automatically Prohibit Employment.

POSITION DESIRED MINIMUM SALARY DESIRED

SCHEDULE PREFERRED
☐ FULL TIME (7 Or More Hours Daily)
☐ PART TIME (3-5 Hours - days)
☐ PART TIME (evenings and weekends)

LIST ALL TIMES YOU ARE AVAILABLE TO WORK

HOW WERE YOU REFERRED TO
☐ EMPLOYEE ☐ AD ☐ AGENCY
☐ OTHER (SPECIFY)

	SUNDAY	MONDAY	TUESDAY	WEDNESDAY	THURSDAY	FRIDAY	SATURDAY
FROM		FROM	FROM	FROM	FROM	FROM	FROM
TO		TO	TO	TO	TO	TO	TO

HAVE YOU EVER APPLIED FOR EMPLOYMENT WITH OR ANY SUBSIDIARY OF ?
IF YES, INDICATE DATE AND LOCATIONS.
☐ YES ☐ NO

HAVE YOU EVER BEEN EMPLOYED BY OR ANY SUBSIDIARY OF ? ☐ YES ☐ NO

IF YOU WERE EMPLOYED, UNDER WHAT NAME WERE YOU EMPLOYED? STORE LOCATION?

RELATIVE IN OUR EMPLOY? NAME DEPARTMENT
☐ YES ☐ NO

FOREIGN LANGUAGES SPOKEN FLUENTLY WHICH WOULD BE HELPFUL IN POSITION SOUGHT.

LIST YOUR INTERESTS, HOBBIES, OR SPECIAL SKILLS

LIST NAMES OF ALL ORGANIZATIONS OF WHICH YOU ARE A MEMBER (EXCLUDE ANY ORGANIZATION WHICH WOULD INDICATE THE FOLLOWING: RACE, COLOR, CREED, ANCESTRY, NATIONAL ORIGIN, RELIGION, SEX, OR MARITAL STATUS.)

PREVIOUS EMPLOYMENT
LIST IN ORDER OF EMPLOYMENT STARTING WITH YOUR PRESENT EMPLOYMENT. PLEASE ACCOUNT FOR ALL TIME, INCLUDING CURRENT EMPLOYMENT, MILITARY SERVICE, PART TIME JOBS, AND PERIODS OF UNEMPLOYMENT. IF YOU HELD TWO JOBS AT THE SAME TIME, BE SURE TO LIST BOTH JOBS. STATE IF ANY OF THESE EMPLOYERS ARE RELATED TO YOU. USE ADDITIONAL SHEET IF NECESSARY.

DATE FROM MO YR	DATE TO MO YR	NAME OF BUSINESS	ADDRESS/PHONE OF BUSINESS	JOB TITLE OR NATURE OF JOB	SALARY START END	REASON FOR LEAVING

PLEASE COMPLETE REVERSE SIDE - DO NOT WRITE BELOW THIS LINE

COMPLETE THIS SECTION ONLY AFTER AN OFFER OF EMPLOYMENT

JOB TITLE SCHEDULE DESCRIPTION (DAYS, HOURS, ETC.) TOTAL NO. DAYS

STORE GROUP/DEPT.# PAYROLL NUMBER HOURLY RATE COMMISSION RATE SCHEDULED HOURS Initial review cycle ☐ 6 MOS./12 MOS.

DATE OF EMPLOYMENT YEAR MONTH DAY TMP. REG. DATE OF BIRTH YEAR MONTH DAY EMPLOYED BY DATE ☐ 9 MOS./18 MOS.

Figure 4–1 Employment application.

EDUCATION

SCHOOL	NAME & ADDRESS OF SCHOOL	COURSE OF STUDY	DATE FROM MO YR	DATE TO MO YR	CIRCLE LAST YEAR COMPLETED				LIST DIPLOMA/DEGREE
HIGH SCHOOL					1	2	3	4	
COLLEGE					1	2	3	4	
OTHER (SPECIFY)					1	2	3	4	

UNITED STATES MILITARY SERVICE RECORD

BRANCH OF SERVICE	DATE INDUCTED	DATE OF SEPARATION OR DISCHARGE	RANK AT DISCHARGE	SERIAL NUMBER

HAVE YOU RECENTLY RECEIVED NOTICE TO REPORT FOR DUTY IN THE ARMED SERVICES? ☐ YES ☐ NO   DESCRIBE SPECIAL TRAINING OR DUTIES

DO YOU HAVE ANY MENTAL OR PHYSICAL HANDICAPS WHICH WOULD PRECLUDE YOU FROM PERFORMING THE JOB FOR WHICH YOU ARE APPLYING? ☐ YES ☐ NO

LIST THE TYPE OF JOBS/PROFESSIONS OF YOUR FRIENDS/RELATIVES (ie: TEACHER, LAWYER, PLUMBER). WHAT WERE THE BEST & WORST FEATURES OF THE JOB?

JOBS OR PROFESSIONS	BEST FEATURES	WORST FEATURES

WHAT ARE THE MOST IMPORTANT THINGS THAT MAKE A COMPANY A GOOD PLACE TO WORK?	WHAT ARE SOME OF THE THINGS YOU DIDN'T LIKE ABOUT JOBS YOU'VE HAD?

IN CASE OF EMERGENCY DURING WORKING HOURS, NOTIFY:

NAME	ADDRESS	TELEPHONE NUMBER

IMPORTANT (PLEASE READ AND SIGN)

The facts set forth in this application are true and correct. I understand that if employed, any false or misleading statements, omissions or failure to fully answer any question will result in my immediate dismissal, regardless of when such information is discovered. I further understand and agree that I may be bonded if employed. I agree to submit myself at any time upon request for medical examination and or testing as permitted by law. I authorize   to secure a consumer report from consumer reporting agencies (i.e. Credit Bureau Inc., Stores Protective Association, etc.), to investigate and verify all information submitted in connection with my application for employment and subsequently as   deems appropriate. Upon written request from me to   I will be informed of the name and address of each consumer reporting agency, if any, from which   has obtained a consumer report relating to me.

I understand and agree that nothing contained in any   handbook, manual, rules or regulations, practice, policy, etc., shall be deemed to create an employment contract between myself and   It is further understood and agreed that my employment relationship with   may be terminated on any day by myself or   for any reason, or no reason, without liability. I represent that I am not relying upon any promises or representations regarding either the nature or duration of my employment in accepting employment if it is offered to me. I understand that no supervisor, manager or other representative of   has any authority to enter into any express or implied contract. I further understand and agree that no promise, representation, inducement or agreement contrary to the above is binding unless it is in writing, expressly states that it is a contract, and is signed by the Chairman of

I CERTIFY THAT I HAVE READ THE ABOVE,
    UNDERSTAND IT AND AGREE TO IT ....

SIGNATURE OF APPLICANT (DO NOT PRINT)

REASON FOR NON-HIRE	☐ MORE QUALIFIED PERSON NECESSARY/HIRED	☐ CANDIDATE NOT INTERESTED IN JOB AVAILABLE GIVE REASON - SALARY, SCHEDULE, ETC.
	☐ NO SUITABLE OPENINGS AT THIS TIME	
	☐ HOLD FOR FURTHER CONSIDERATION (one month)	INTERVIEWER'S INITIALS AND DATE

Figure 4–1 *(continued)*

Bonding Form

The use of a bonding form need not mean that the employee will in fact be bonded. Simply having the applicant fill out a bonding form, even if it is never submitted to a bonding company, serves several purposes. The use of a bonding form that contains many of the same questions as the application is strongly recommended, whether or not an actual bond is issued. We recommend that the bonding form be filled out only after the applicant has been hired because it is then permissible to ask the date and place of the employee's birth. This information is required for employee pensions and retirement benefits.

Additionally, if the bonding form is completed some time after the employment application and if it asks for the same information as the application, the employer can compare the answers given on each form. Applicants who lie or make up information on employment applications frequently cannot remember the false information they have given. They therefore give different answers to similar questions on the bonding form. This discrepancy provides a legitimate avenue of inquiry. If it is found that the employee gave false answers on the application, then grounds for termination exist, provided that the appropriate language was used on the application and that it was properly acknowledged and signed by the applicant.

Bonding forms have one other advantage: Many applicants tend to be more honest when answering such questions as "Have you ever been convicted of a crime?" or "Have you ever been discharged from a job?" when they appear on the bonding form. This occurs because applicants believe that a bonding company will verify the information on the form, and they therefore tend to be more honest than when filling out the employment application. See Figure 4–2 for a sample bonding form.

Employment Interview

Every applicant who is basically qualified for the position and who appears otherwise qualified (by virtue of stature, appearance, or language) should be given a thorough interview. The interview is designed to develop in-depth information about the applicant's background and skills, as well as some indication of his or her character and motivation. A good interviewer asks open-ended questions that allow the applicant to speak at length rather than questions that can be answered simply "Yes" or "No." Hypothetical situations related to the job under consideration will illuminate how the applicant would handle similar situations on the job. A word of caution about interviewing applicants: Beware of asking discriminatory questions. Discriminatory questions are those that relate to such issues as religion, age, ethnic background, and arrest record, as outlined in Figure 4–3.

It is a good idea to keep written notes of significant answers or reactions to the interview, and it is recommended that at least two people interview each applicant. Two interviews by different people help eliminate unconscious biases and the tendency to hire applicants who reflect one interviewer's likes or match preconceptions of the ideal applicant.

BONDING INFORMATION
PLEASE PRINT

OFFICE USE ONLY

STORE _____
(NAME)

FULL
NAME _____   SOC.
                                                  SEC. # _____
COMPLETE   (LAST)   (FIRST)   (MIDDLE)
ADDRESS _____

PHONE NO. _____   HOW LONG AT
                              THIS ADDRESS? _____   HOW LONG IN
                                                           AREA? _____

PREVIOUS ADDRESS _____   HOW LONG? _____

MARITAL STATUS—
MARRIED ☐ DIVORCED ☐   PLACE OF BIRTH _____   DATE OF BIRTH _____
WIDOW(ER) ☐ SINGLE ☐   DRIVER'S
                        LICENSE NO. _____ OR OTHER I.D.
                                                         (TYPE & NO.) _____

NAME OF SPOUSE, PARENTS (IF LIVING), OR OTHER NEAREST RELATIVE

NAME	RELATION	ADDRESS	EMPLOYER	POSITION

HAVE YOU EVER USED ANOTHER NAME? _____ IF YES, WHAT NAME AND WHEN? _____

HAVE YOU EVER BEEN BONDED? _____ IF YES, WHERE WERE YOU WORKING? _____

HAVE YOU EVER BEEN REFUSED A BOND? _____ IF YES, EXPLAIN: _____
_____   DATE _____   PLACE _____

HAVE YOU EVER BEEN CONVICTED OF A CRIME? _____ IF YES, ☐ FELONY ☐ MISDEMEANOR

EXPLAIN: _____   DATE _____   PLACE _____

HAVE YOU EVER BEEN DISCHARGED FROM A POSITION? _____ IF YES, EXPLAIN: _____
_____   DATE _____   PLACE _____

PLEASE ACCOUNT FOR ALL TIME SINCE LEAVING SCHOOL, INCLUDING CURRENT EMPLOYMENT, MILITARY SERVICE AND PERIODS OF UNEMPLOYMENT. STATE IF ANY OF THESE EMPLOYERS ARE RELATED TO YOU.

DATES EMPLOYED MONTH AND YEAR	Name/Address, City and State of Previous Employer(s) Show present or last employer first.	SUPERVISOR AND YOUR JOB TITLE	REASON FOR LEAVING
FROM:			
TO:			
FROM:			
TO:			
FROM:			
TO:			

I HAVE VERIFIED THE BIRTH DATE OF THIS EMPLOYEE PERSONALLY WITNESSING THE DOCUMENT SO NOTED.

PRIMARY
☐ Birth Certificate

SECONDARY SOURCE *(Need One)*
☐ Church Record   ☐ Passport
☐ Entry in Bible   ☐ Life Insurance Policy
☐ Census Certificate   (One in force at least
                         5 years)

SECONDARY SOURCE *(Need Two)*
☐ Relative's Affidavit   ☐ School Verification
☐ Marriage Certificate   ☐ Will or Testament Entry
☐ Military Record   ☐ Naturalization Papers

_____   _____/_____   _____/_____
WITNESSED BY   TITLE   DATE

DO NOT WRITE IN THIS SPACE

DEPT. NAME	STAFF NO.
HOURS	CREDIT DEPT.
SECURITY DEPT.	SPA.

I HEREBY CERTIFY THAT ALL ANSWERS TO THE ABOVE QUESTIONS ARE TRUE AND COMPLETE. I FULLY UNDERSTAND THAT ANY FALSE ANSWERS WILL RESULT IN DISMISSAL OR DENIAL OF EMPLOYMENT.

_____   _____
(SIGNATURE OF APPLICANT)   (DATE)

WHITE . . . . PERSONNEL FILE
YELLOW . . . . CREDIT DEPT.
PINK . . . . SECURITY DEPT.

Figure 4–2 Bonding form.

Pre-Employment Inquiry Guidelines

ACCEPTABLE	SUBJECT	UNACCEPTABLE
Name "Have you ever used another name? /or/ "Is any additional information relative to change of name, use of an assumed name, or nickname necessary to enable a check on your work and education record? If yes, please explain."	**NAME**	Maiden name.
Place of residence.	**RESIDENCE**	"Do you own or rent your home?"
Statement that hire is subject to verification that applicant meets legal age requirements. "If hired can you show proof of age?" "Are you over eighteen years of age?" "If under eighteen, can you, after employment, submit a work permit?"	**AGE**	Age. Birthdate. Dates of attendance or completion of elementary or high school. Questions which tend to identify applicants over age 40.
"Can you, after employment, submit verification of your legal right to work in the United States?" /or/ Statement that such proof may be required after employment.	**BIRTHPLACE, CITIZENSHIP**	Birthplace of applicant, applicant's parents. spouse, or other relatives. "Are you a U.S. citizen?" /or/ Citizenship of applicant. applicant's parents. spouse. or other relatives. Requirements that applicant produce naturalization, first papers. or alien card *prior to employment.*
Languages applicant reads, speaks, or writes, if use of a language other than English is relevant to the job for which applicant is applying.	**NATIONAL ORIGIN**	Questions as to nationality, lineage, ancestry. national origin, descent, or parentage of applicant, applicant's parents, or spouse "What is your mother tongue?" /or/ Language commonly used by applicant. How applicant acquired ability to read, write. or speak a foreign language.
Name and address of parent or guardian if applicant is a minor. Statement of company policy regarding work assignment of employees who are related.	**SEX, MARITAL STATUS, FAMILY**	Questions which indicate applicant's sex. Questions which indicate applicant's marital status. Number and/or ages of children or dependents. Provisions for child care. Questions regarding pregnancy. child bearing. or birth control. Name or address of relative, spouse, or children of adult applicant. "With whom do you reside?" /or/ "Do you live with your parents?"
	RACE, COLOR	Questions as to applicant's race or color. Questions regarding applicant's complexion or color of skin, eyes, hair.

Figure 4–3 Pre-employment inquiring guidelines. (Source: Courtesy of Krout and Schneider, Inc., 1541 Wilshire Boulevard, Suite 200, Los Angeles, CA 90017.)

Pre-Employment Inquiry Guidelines

ACCEPTABLE	SUBJECT	UNACCEPTABLE
Statement that photograph may be required after employment.	PHYSICAL DESCRIPTION, PHOTO-GRAPH	Questions as to applicant's height and weight. Require applicant to affix a photograph to application. Request applicant, at his or her option, to submit a photograph. Require a photograph after interview but before employment.
Statement by employer that offer may be made contingent on applicant passing a job-related physical examination. "Do you have any physical condition or handicap which may limit your ability to perform the job applied for? If yes, what can be done to accommodate your limitation?"	PHYSICAL CONDITION, HANDICAP	Questions regarding applicant's general medical condition, state of health, or illnesses. Questions regarding receipt of Workers' Compensation. "Do you have any physical disabilities or handicaps?"
Statement by employer of regular days, hours, or shifts to be worked.	RELIGION	Questions regarding applicant's religion. Religious days observed /or/ "Does your religion prevent you from working weekends or holidays?"
"Have you ever been convicted of a felony?" Such a question must be accompanied by a statement that a conviction will not necessarily disqualify an applicant from employment.	ARREST, CRIMINAL RECORD	Arrest record /or/ "Have you ever been arrested?"
Statement that bonding is a condition of hire.	BONDING	Questions regarding refusal or cancellation of bonding.
Questions regarding relevant skills acquired during applicant's U.S. military service.	MILITARY SERVICE	General questions regarding military services such as dates, and type of discharge. Questions regarding service in a foreign military.
	ECONOMIC STATUS	Questions regarding applicant's current or past assets, liabilities, or credit rating, including bankruptcy or garnishment.
"Please list job-related organizations, clubs, professional societies, or other associations to which you belong—you may omit those which indicate your race, religious creed, color, national origin, ancestry, sex, or age."	ORGANIZA-TIONS, ACTIVITIES	"List all organizations, clubs, societies, and lodges to which you belong."
"By whom were you referred for a position here?" Names of persons willing to provide professional and/or character references for applicant.	REFERENCES	Questions of applicant's former employers or acquaintances which elicit information specifying the applicant's race, color, religious creed, national origin, ancestry, physical handicap, medical condition, marital status, age, or sex.
Name and address of person to be notified in case of accident or emergency.	NOTICE IN CASE OF EMERGENCY	Name and address of relative to be notified in case of accident or emergency.

Figure 4–3 *(continued)*

It should go without saying that no applicant should ever be summarily rejected because of gender or ethnic or religious background. In large retail environments especially, female security agents are not only desirable but essential. Only female employees can enter women's fitting rooms, they blend in most easily with the majority of customers, and they generally handle confrontational situations better than most men. In our experience, some of the best security agents have been from ethnic minorities. Unconscious bias or preconceptions must be avoided to preclude eliminating a potentially superior employee.

According to a national security newsletter, [14] trained interviewers can effectively screen applicants for honesty. This reference cites "integrity interviewing," a technique taught by John E. Reid & Associates of Chicago, as a tool that can be adapted to a wide variety of hiring needs. Integrity interviewing provides the interviewer with the skills to detect and reject dishonest or drug-addicted applicants. An outline entitled *Interviewing Techniques for Hiring the Best Security Candidate,* which covers key points relating to this subject, is part of training course material offered by Wicklander-Zulawski & Associates, Inc. [15] See Appendix A at the end of this chapter.

Suggested Interview Questions

In addition to the interviewing outline, Wicklander & Zulawski have developed 28 suggested interview questions that could provide meaningful direction for interviewers:

1. Why do you want to leave your present employer?
2. What do you like most about your present company?
3. What do you like least about your present company, i.e., policy, structure?
4. What frustrated you most?
5. What did you personally enjoy the most?
6. What is the current shrinkage? If not known, why?
7. What are the company's annual sales?
8. What is the highest shrinkage department? What are the contributing factors?
9. What percent of your shrinkage is due to internal theft, shoplifting, and paperwork?
10. What are some examples of internal theft cases you have seen? What steps led up to developing this case? What was your favorite case?
11. Who conducts these interviews? How do you feel about that?
12. What training have you received in apprehending shoplifters, conducting interviews, safety, etc.? What did you think of the training you received?
13. Have you ever testified before?
14. How many lawsuits have you been involved in? How many bad stops have you made? What caused this to occur? What could be done differently?
15. What experience do you have with closed-circuit television?
16. Have you ever given any training to a large group?
17. What types of audits have you done or been involved in? How do you feel about auditing?

18. What types of exception reports does your company use? How are they formatted? What do you do with the information? How do you plot the information?
19. Do you have an in-store reward program? What do you do to encourage participation?
20. What is your store's refund policy? How do you like it?
21. What kind of interaction do you have with store management or corporate department heads?
22. What types of reports do you write? How much time do you have to do them? How soon after the incident must the report be written?
23. How organized do you find yourself to be? In what areas could you be more organized?
24. What do you want to gain from this company?
25. Where do you want to be in three to five years?
26. What do you do when you are unable to change things you feel are important to change?
27. What do you believe are your strengths? Weaknesses?
28. Upon doing a complete background investigation on you, what would be the most positive and negative feedback we would receive?

Honesty Tests

At least 50 different so-called honesty tests or pencil and paper polygraph tests are available today.[16] The makers of these tests claim that they can identify applicants who have an above average tendency to be dishonest, thus permitting an employer to screen them out during the selection process. Before using any of these tests, they should be cleared with legal counsel. Any test used must be properly validated to avoid legal ramifications. Many of the available tests have withstood legal challenges, but some states (e.g., Massachusetts) have outlawed them, and there is legislation pending in other states that would limit or prohibit their use.

Personality Tests

A variety of personality tests is available, and some employers use them to screen applicants. One of the oldest and most popular is the Minnesota Multiphasic Personality Inventory (MMPI), which is reported to be able to detect over aggressiveness and psychosis, among other personality traits. This test is quite popular with police departments[17] (Boston, Chicago, Detroit, and New York City use this test) and some security services companies. However, in 1990 one retailer who used a version of this test to screen security employees was held to be in violation of California's privacy and labor laws by a California Court of Appeal and was enjoined from further use of the test.[18]

Polygraph

The use of a polygraph—more popularly known as a *lie detector*—for screening employment applicants has for all intents and purposes been outlawed by the Employee Polygraph Protection Act of 1988. Although a few exceptions to the general prohibition of polygraph pre-employment screening do exist, they are so limited that they are not of concern here.

Graphology

Handwriting analysis has been of interest for centuries to those who study human behavior. Although some evidence suggests that handwriting can predict future behavior, especially honesty, this field of study has not been scientifically validated to the point where it can be safely recommended as a pre-employment screening device.[19] Nonetheless it is an investigative tool, and we have seen some startling results of its use.

Drug Testing

Drug testing, whether of applicants or employees, is an extremely controversial issue, and it has been the subject of numerous legal challenges, much litigation, and some legislation. Advocates and opponents of testing can both produce credible evidence supporting their point of view. Again, as with most employment issues encountered today, competent legal counsel should be sought before beginning a drug testing program. Federal and local laws currently exist that regulate and limit drug testing, and the entire matter is undergoing constant change. Any drug testing program must be well conceptualized and properly executed, and it must contain appropriate checks and balances and quality controls.

Background Investigation

The topic of background investigations, whether conducted before or after employment, is a complex one. Numerous financial and legal factors must be taken into consideration before decisions are made. The issue of cost is certainly a primary consideration; background investigations that go beyond a few local telephone calls are relatively expensive. Any background investigation worth its name can easily cost the equivalent of an in-house investigator's salary for one day. The cost of investigating an applicant who has moved frequently, has an out-of-state residence, or has a lengthy prior employment history can exceed a week's salary. However, it's money well spent!

What should a background investigation include? We suggest that the following areas be investigated and verified: education, prior employment, current address, criminal and civil court records, and driving records (for employees who will use vehicles on company business). We will discuss each of these areas of investigation separately, indicating why they are important and what can be learned from them.

Candidates applying for sensitive jobs—such as positions that provide access to cash or sensitive information, uncontrolled access to property, merchandise, or other assets, or positions that are by their very nature executive or policy making—should be subjected to additional investigation of their credit history and financial and property holdings. Thorough interviews with the candidate's references are also highly desirable. For entry-level security applicants, the more thorough the investigation, the better. Security agents can cost their employers hundreds of thousands —perhaps millions—of dollars should they make a serious blunder in judgment or action.

Education

Anecdotical reports indicate that over 60% of all job candidates provide some untruthful information on their employment application. Other government and private studies indicate that up to 25% of job applicant resumes contain outright lies and falsehoods. [20] One of the areas most frequently lied about on resumes and applications is the level of education achieved by the job seeker. Applicants who attended college but never formally graduated frequently claim that they received a degree. Even if the applicant would have been just as favorably considered without a degree, his or her character and sense of truthfulness is certainly brought into question by the fabrication. Here's a hint: When interviewing an applicant who claims to have a degree, a good question to ask is, "If we required it, could you bring a copy of your diploma or transcript or otherwise furnish proof of your graduation?" A quick, affirmative answer tends to confirm the applicant's claim. If the applicant seems hesitant, you might question whether the applicant really has a degree.

Prior Employment

Verifying prior employment is important because a person's past behavior is a good indicator of his or her future behavior. An applicant whose prior job history is exemplary will probably remain an excellent employee; similarly, an applicant who has had problems with former employers will probably continue to have employment-related problems. Verifying prior employment, in addition to establishing whether the applicant was in fact gainfully employed as claimed may also produce clues as to the applicant's character, abilities, and attitudes. These clues will assist the employer in making a good decision. Therefore, when verifying former employment, to the extent possible, verify not only dates of employment, positions held, salary, and performance but also information relating to character, attitude, and other skills or areas of legitimate concern.

Unfortunately, since the mid-1980s, employers have been increasingly less willing to reveal information about former employees. The fear of lawsuits for invasion of privacy, defamation, and other torts has essentially limited former employers to providing only the dates of employment, position held, and sometimes the rate of pay or salary. This limited response to requests for information applies even when you have waivers or letters of authorization from the applicant. Occasionally, if someone in authority with the former employer is known by someone at the inquiring company, additional information can be obtained "off the record," but this type of information must be used judiciously, and the confidence under which it was obtained cannot be breached.

In 1989 a new form of civil damage claim against former employers arose. These civil suits are filed when an employee—who would not have been hired had the former employer revealed derogatory but truthful information about the applicant during a pre-employment inquiry—creates a civil liability for his or her current employer. The current employer sues the former employer for damages, alleging that the former employer was negligent in not having provided the disqualifying information about the employee. One such case involved a stockbroker who defrauded his clients and was terminated by his firm. The firm did not disclose this information when queried by the broker's prospective new employer. The broker was subsequently hired and defrauded the clients of his new employer. After his prior history was discovered, the broker's last employer sued his former employer for not disclosing his prior misconduct during a pre-employment check. The former employer, of course, claimed privacy concerns and fear of a defamation action. This situation is a classic example of the old adage, "You're damned if you do and damned if you don't."

Current Address

Appicants' current addresses are needed to verify other aspects of their background. In addition, it is required for official company records and for withholding taxes.

Criminal Records

Nearly one in 10 Americans has a criminal record of some sort; failure to check criminal files means that you have a one in 10 chance of hiring someone with a criminal past.

In most jurisdictions, it is no longer possible to obtain criminal history information, either arrest records (which are illegal to use) or conviction records, directly from state or local police agencies. Conviction information is available through the county clerk's office. The use of conviction records to deny employment must be reasonably applied. Federal rulings have held that the conviction must be relevant to the position for which the applicant is being considered and that the length of time since the conviction and the age of the applicant at the time of the conviction must be taken into consideration. A single teenage joy-riding conviction would not likely disqualify a 30-year-old applicant; however, an adult petty theft (shoplifting) conviction would likely disqualify an applicant for any security position and would certainly be a major consideration for any retail position.

Some states do permit direct inquiry into state criminal justice records when the inquiry concerns applicants for security positions. For example, California enacted a new law in January 1991 that allows prospective employers to submit the fingerprints of job applicants for security positions directly to the state for a criminal records check. A few other states have similar procedures.

Civil Court Records

State and federal civil records often provide detailed financial, employment, and personal information about applicants. Serious problems such as theft occasionally appear in civil files and not in criminal files; this often happens when former employers seek redress for theft losses through the civil courts rather than through the criminal justice system. Credit problems, divorces, and other interpersonal disputes are frequently disclosed through civil court filings.

Driving Records

For applicants who will drive a company vehicle or a personal vehicle on company business, a driving record check is mandatory. Accidents, driving under the influence, speeding, and traffic or parking tickets will all appear in these records. The applicant's prior failure to carry insurance (in those states with mandatory financial responsibility laws) can also be uncovered. Can you imagine the liability of an employer for negligent hiring if a security guard, while on patrol and driving a company vehicle, becomes intoxicated and kills a pedestrian, and then it is discovered that the employee has a history of reckless and drunk driving? Driving records can often also verify addresses, previous employment, and date of birth.

Other Records and Sources of Information

References.   Although listed references are not normally verified for most applicants for employment, it is considered essential for security applicants. Talking with people who know the applicant can be illuminating. Surprisingly, even references provided by the applicant—people who would be expected to be favorable in their comments about the applicant—occasionally disclose derogatory or disqualifying information. References can often verify aspects of an applicant's background that cannot otherwise be verified. It is essential when talking with references that any statements made in confidence be respected. A face-to-face interview with references produces better information than attempting to conduct an interview over the telephone, although telephone interviews sometimes cannot be avoided.

Consider the liability of a store owner whose security agent uses excessive force in apprehending a suspected shoplifter, seriously injuring the suspect in the process. A lawsuit uncovers that this security agent has a history of violence and a reputation for overaggressiveness, which could have been uncovered by interviewing references. Would you want to be that security agents' employer?

One of the primary benefits derived from interviewing references is the ability to obtain what are frequently referred to as *developed references* or *throw-offs*. Developed references are people who the listed references tell you also know the applicant well. Developed references, because they are not suggested by the applicant, will frequently be more candid about the applicant's true character and personality. Depending on the sensitivity of the position and the results of several listed and developed reference interviews, the investigator may want to go one level further and obtain second-generation references from the developed references. Rarely does a routine pre-employment background investigation go beyond the second level of developed references.

Credit Reports. Credit reports can contain valuable financial and biographical information and are a valuable source for pre-employment screening. Credit reports, however, are regulated by Public Law 91-508, also known as Section 604 of the Fair Credit Reporting Act. This law proscribes the legal uses of and access to consumer credit information. A listing of these restrictions is contained in *The Employer's Guide to Pre-Employment Screening and Background Investigations* and is reproduced in Appendix B at the end of this chapter.

Special Records. Although the entry-level security applicant's pre-employment background screening may never require consulting any information sources other than those already discussed, we would be remiss if we did not mention other sources that may occasionally be consulted. These sources are simply listed below with a brief description of the type of information they contain.

Bankruptcy Records: Found in U.S. Bankruptcy Courts in federal courthouses, these records list bankruptcy filings.

Tax Records: These county tax assessor files contain property and personal tax records that are open to the public.

Business Information: Sources such as Dun & Bradstreet, Dow Jones, and Standard & Poor's contain financial and ownership information regarding private and publicly held companies.

Fictitious Name Files: Most county offices maintain files on fictitious or assumed names used by businesses in that jurisdiction. These files show the true names of the owners.

Corporation Commissioner Files: Each state's Secretary of State's office usually has a file showing the listed principals and owners of businesses incorporated in the state.

Newspaper Morgues: Newspaper files can be checked if the approximate date of an item is known. Some files are indexed by subject.

Professional Associations: The membership or certification of professionals—for example, attorneys, certified public accountants (CPAs), registered engineers, and registered stock brokers—can often be verified by consulting professional associations such as the local Bar Association.

Trade Associations: Many union and trade associations can verify the membership of certain individuals, such as musicians and bartenders.

On-line Data Services: Many databases in existence today can for a fee provide information about a variety of topics. Some private detective agencies maintain memberships in many of these databases. Although it is somewhat dated, the book *Where's What—Sources of Information for Federal Investigators*[21] provides help in uncovering the source of all sorts of information, and it lists databases that may prove useful when conducting background investigations.

SUMMARY

Merchants have an awesome responsibility in selecting the security employees whose daily performance will affect the lives of other human beings and the reputation and economic health of the organization. The failure to recognize the magnitude of this responsibility can lead to negligent hiring litigation.

Candidates for employment have qualities, characteristics, strengths, and perhaps problems that must be determined. A key vehicle for discovering those assets or liabilities is the application for employment. The application must be carefully examined for indicators of deception. Comparing a bond form to the employment application is one sound strategy. Background investigations, including verification of prior employment, is most important. Interviewing the applicant is necessary, and investigating unexplained periods of employment, unanswered questions, and any unusual or conflicting information is essential.

The task of the professional security administrator or informed retail manager is to do everything within reason to preclude selecting people who create questionable situations. If a problem does arise and a complaint is received, the resultant careful scrutiny of the employee must not reveal derogatory information in the employee's background or negligence in his or her selection.

NOTES

1. *Hayes Report on Loss Prevention,* vol. 2, no. 3, (Summer 1987) p. 2. Published by Jack L. Hayes International, Inc., Stanfordville, NY.
2. *Labor and Unemployment Update,* no. 98-3 (March 27, 1989). Published by Orrick, Herrington & Sutcliffe, San Francisco, CA.
3. Norman D. Bates, "Understanding the Liability of Negligent Hiring," *Security Management* (July 1990), suppl. Published by the American Society for Industrial Security.
4. Arthur J. Bilek, John C. Klotter, and R. Keegan Federal, *Legal Aspects of Private Security* (Cincinnati: Anderson Publishing Company, 1981), p. 29.
5. National Advisory Committee on Criminal Justice Standards and Goals, *Private Security: Report of the Task Force on Private Security,* Stock #052-003-00225-6 (Washington, D.C.: U.S. Government Printing Office, 1976).
6. See note 5 *supra,* pp. 80 and 81.
7. Safeway Stores v. Kelley, 448A 2nd 856 (1982).
8. Sorrel Wildhorn, *Private Police in the United States: Findings and Recommendations,* vols. I–V (Washington, D.C.: Rand Corporation and U.S. Government Printing Office, 1972).
9. See note 5 *supra,* p. 65.
10. Care must be taken not to violate any of the provisions of the Americans with Disabilities Act (ADA), which was signed into law on July 26, 1990.
11. Asking for the applicant's date or place of birth is considered under federal rulings to be potentially discriminatory and is prohibited prior to actual hire.
12. Asking for any arrest record is considered potentially discriminatory and is prohibited under federal rulings.
13. See note 10 *supra.*

14. The April 1990 issue of *Corporate Security* contains a detailed discussion of the Reid integrity interview and a general review of applicant interviewing. *Corporate Security* is published monthly by Business Research Publications, Inc., 817 Broadway, New York, NY 10003.

15. Wicklander-Zulawski & Associates, Inc., One Woodfield Lake, Suite 139, Schaumberg, IL 60173, phone 1-800-222-7789. Doug Wicklander and Dave Zulawski present seminars across the United States on interview and interrogation techniques for security and personnel executives and practitioners.

16. For a review, see R. Michael O'Bannon, Linda A. Goldinger, and Gavin S. Appleby, *Honesty and Integrity Testing: A Practical Guide* (Atlanta: Applied Information Resources, 1989).

17. "What You Don't Know Can Hurt You," *The Lipman Report* (May 15, 1990). Published by Guardsmark, Inc., Memphis, TN 38103.

18. *Sibi Soroka et al. v. Dayton Hudson Corp.*, 91 *Daily Journal* D.A.R. 13204 (1991).

19. For a discussion on graphology as a pre-employment screening tool, see *Security Letter*, vol. XX, no. 15, Part I (August 15, 1990), p. 2. Published by Security Letter, Inc., 166 East 96th Street, New York, NY 10128.

20. *Security Management* magazine special preemployment screening supplement, July 1990, "Screening for Success" page 13A, article entitled "I Screen, You Screen" by Edmund J. Pankau, CPP. *Security Management* is a publication of the American Society for Industrial Security, 1655 North Fort Myer Dr., Suite 1200, Arlington, VA 22209.

21. Harry J. Murphy, *Where's What—Sources of Information for Federal Investigators* (Quadrangle/The New York Times Book Company, N.Y., 1976).

APPENDIX A

Interviewing Techniques for Hiring the Best Security Candidate

I. RECOGNIZING THE NEED FOR EFFECTIVE INTERVIEWING
   A. Liability for negligent hiring
   B. Proper hiring adds to acceptability of loss prevention department
   C. Several hiring tools are taken away (e.g., polygraph, some forms of testing)
   D. Ineffective interviewing means probable vacancies in the future; poor selection will result in terminations, which create future openings, a vicious cycle
      1. Costly
      2. Lost productivity
      3. More difficult to replace due to dwindling work force
II. WHY UNQUALIFIED OR UNDESIRABLE PEOPLE ARE HIRED
   A. Failed to establish necessary skills to do the job
   B. Failed to ask the right questions to see if applicant possessed the proper skills and personality traits
   C. Applicant misrepresented self
   D. Fell into the "warm body syndrome" (hiring someone to fill a position without regard to the qualification or fitness for the position. They were alive, hence a "warm body")

Source: Courtesy of Wicklander-Zulawski & Associates, Inc., 555 East Butterfield Road, Suite 302, Lombard, IL 60148.

III. IDENTIFY THE JOB DESCRIPTION
    A. Identify and prioritize responsibilities from your perspective and that of people in that position
        1. Apprehend shoplifters
        2. Conduct investigations
        3. Conduct employee interviews
        4. Conduct in-store training
        5. Be involved in prevention programs
        6. Be responsible for supervising others
        7. Prepare budgets
        8. Travel

IV. IDENTIFY SKILLS NECESSARY TO PERFORM RESPONSIBILITIES
    A. Ability to "read" people and blend in
    B. Ability to approach and talk with strangers
    C. Detail oriented
    D. Good organizational skills
    E. Good communicator
    F. Good interviewer
    G. Good with math
    H. Leader

V. IDENTIFY PERSONALITY TRAITS NECESSARY TO PERFORM JOB
    A. Look at personality of management and direct supervisor
    B. Look at personality and experience level of associates reporting to the position to be filled
    C. What is the philosophy of the department?
        1. Apprehension
        2. Prevention
        3. Prosecution
        4. Restitution
    D. What is the corporate environment like?
        1. Strong central management
        2. Loose environment
        3. Hands-on management vs. delegation

VI. EVALUATE PRIOR SUCCESSES AND FAILURES
    A. Evaluate and target information elements of best performers in the position (take successful employees and identify why they are successful; seek similar attributes in applicants)
    B. Evaluate why an individual was not successful in a position and identify the cause of failure
        1. Personality
        2. Management style
        3. Skills
        4. Difference of philosophy
    C. If the position is open due to resignation, identify the cause
        1. Hours

        2. Travel
        3. Legitimate personality conflicts
        4. Stagnation of career path
        5. Salary
        6. Pressure
        7. Difference of philosophy
        8. Supervisor not accessible
        9. Did not like direction of company
    D. If the position is open due to termination, identify the cause
        1. Lack of skills
        2. Poor productivity
        3. Lack of honesty and integrity
        4. Counterproductive behavior
VII. DETERMINE AND ORGANIZE WHAT YOU WANT TO KNOW REGARDING THE APPLICANT
VIII. REVIEW RESUME
 IX. CONDUCT THE INTERVIEW
    A. Recognize how applicants misrepresent themselves during an interview
        1. Exaggeration
        2. Fabrication
        3. Minimization
        4. Omission
        5. Deceptive denials
    B. Recognize why applicants misrepresent themselves
        1. You have told the applicant too much about the company at the beginning
        2. You were too formal during the interview, thus stifling interaction and openness
        3. The applicant tried to be perfect for the job
    C. Techniques for encouraging truthfulness
        1. Adopt a nonthreatening attitude
        2. Ask nonthreatening questions
        3. Briefly explain the position
        4. Explain how the selection process will take place
        5. Ease into the importance of truthfulness
        6. Give an overview of the areas you will be discussing

APPENDIX B

Restrictions on the Use of and Access to Consumer Credit Reports

Section 604 of the Fair Credit Reporting Act (also known as Public Law 91-508) details the permissible uses and access of consumer credit reports. It specifically states that a consumer reporting agency may furnish a consumer report under the following circumstances and no other:

1. In response to the order of a court having jurisdiction to issue such an order.
2. In accordance with the written instructions of the consumer to whom it relates.
3. To a person who the employer has reason to believe:
   a. intends to use the information in connection with a transaction involving the consumer on whom the information is to be furnished and involving the extension of credit to, or review or collection of, an account of the consumer; or
   b. intends to use the information for employment purposes; or
   c. intends to use the information in connection with the underwriting of insurance involving the consumer; or
   d. intends to use the information in connection with the consumer's eligibility for a license or other benefit granted by a government instrumentality

---

Source: Courtesy of Krout and Schneider, Inc., 1541 Wilshire Boulevard, Suite 200, Los Angeles, CA 90017.

required by law to consider an applicant's financial responsibility or status; or

e. otherwise has a legitimate business need for the information in connection with a business transaction involving the consumer.

While the federal law (Section 604 of the FCRA) does not require the employer to obtain the applicant's permission prior to obtaining a consumer credit report, some states do have such requirements. New York, for example, requires prior notification to the applicant of the employer's intent to secure a consumer credit report and California, by enacting Assembly Bill 1102, which became law on January 1, 1992, mandates that employers must give written notice to anyone on whom a consumer credit report will be obtained for "employment purposes" prior to obtaining such a report.

5

Training Security Personnel

The training of new security employees is just as important as the screening of applicants before hiring—and for an essentially similar reason. Just as negligent hiring has become a common tort, so has negligent training. It is easy to understand the allegation in the following cause of action (listed in a civil complaint for damages): The employer knew or should have known that the assignment, supervision, training or retention of an employee was likely to cause damage to another person. In other words, the employer should have known that an untrained or improperly trained store detective charged with the responsibility of detaining and arresting members of the public could injure someone.

If security employees, whose unique duties and the possibility that their work will result in physical or psychological injury to others, are not properly trained and supervised, civil liability is almost inevitable. A thorough discussion of these torts and the civil liability of security personnel in general is found in *Private Security and the Law*,[1] a book devoted exclusively to the legal aspects of private security. We also examine these subjects in Chapter 11.

What degree of training is required not only to minimize civil liability but also to ensure an effective, efficient, and productive security officer? Perhaps the answer lies in the definition of training itself.

TRAINING DEFINED

The training function means different things to different people; it is widely misunderstood. Certainly there is a question of definition, and a typical dictionary definition *(Webster's)* tells us little when it describes training in this manner:

training. *Noun.* Act, process, or method of one who trains; state of being trained. *Adjective.* That trains; used in or for training: as, a *training* ship for sailors.

Even aside from its obvious circularity, what does this explanation really explain? Is it any wonder there is confusion? A more workable definition might be the following:

> *Training is an educational, informative, skill-development process that brings about anticipated performance through a change in comprehension and behavior.*

Basically, management wants the employees to know three things. It is important for them to understand

1. what management wants them to do
2. why management wants them to do it
3. how management wants it done

"POP" FORMULA: POLICY, OBJECTIVES AND PROCEDURES

The *what, why,* and *how* are related to *policy, objectives,* and *procedures.* From this correlation we have developed the POP Training Formula, a three-tier formula for job training.

The Objective tier in Figure 5–1 deserves special attention. Too frequently the training process overlooks the necessity of informing employees *why* this should be done and *why* that should not be done. When employees are informed about the why's, their performance will improve. This point cannot be overemphasized.

Readers who are familiar with the *who, what, where, how, why,* and *when* investigative formula may wonder what has happened to the *who, when,* and *where*. The *who* (the employee who is being trained) is obviously implied, and the *when* and *where*, in this context, are included in the *how*.

Now let's translate the POP Formula into training for a specific job, such as shoplifting detective. Re-examining the suggested definition, it is clear that there

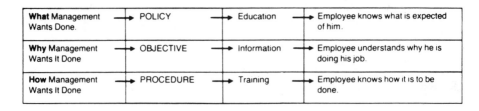

Figure 5–1 The POP formula for training. (Source: Charles A. Sennewald, *Effective Security Management* [Stoneham, Mass.: Butterworths, 1985].)

are three aspects of training: education, information, and skill development. The example in Figure 5–2 makes it apparent that, of the three tiers of the formula, the Procedure tier addresses itself to skill development and the other two tiers, Policy and Objective, are educational and informative in nature. It is not enough for detectives to know that management's policy is to arrest and prosecute every shoplifter. They must also understand the objectives that make this policy reasonable and necessary, and they must thoroughly grasp the various procedures that are essential in the detectives' execution of their responsibilities. The proper combination of education, information, and skill development round out and give substance and definition to *training*.

TYPES OF TRAINING

With this concept of training in mind, coupled with the philosophy that training is an ongoing process that aims at maintaining a level of understanding and performance in keeping with the evolution of modern society, let's examine the various types of training that may be pursued. They include the following:

- basic training
- on-the-job training
- telephone training
- training bulletins
- roll-call training
- subscription training

	COMPANY PROGRAM	EMPLOYEE FUNCTION
POLICY (What Management Wants Done)	Arrest and prosecute every shoplifter.	Has been hired by the company to specifically detect and apprehend shoplifters.
OBJECTIVE (Why Management Wants It done)	Reduce shoplifting losses. Deter others by example of arrests. Punish or discourage offenders.	• Helps to reduce losses caused by shoplifting. • Deters others from shoplifting. • Helps to punish offenders through the criminal justice system.
PROCEDURE (How Management Wants It Done)	Lawful gathering of the necessary evidence to justify arrest and support prosecution of shoplifters.	• Sees customer approach merchandise. • Sees customer select merchandise. • Sees secretion of merchandise. • Sees that no payment is made. • Sees removal of merchandise from store. • Approaches customer and says, "Excuse me, etc." • Carries out arrest with justification. • Makes written report of incident, etc.

Figure 5–2 The POP formula for shoplifting detective training. (Source: Charles A. Sennewald, *Effective Security Management* [Stoneham, Mass.: Butterworths, 1985].)

- interactive video training
- seminars and workshop training

Basic Training

Basic training is best accomplished in a structured, formal classroom setting where the new security officers can concentrate and apply their full attention to the matter at hand. Basic training can consist of a variety of topics,[3] but the list below provides a minimum foundation for the responsibilities of a security officer who works in a public environment and comes into frequent contact with the public (as opposed to a guard who patrols the exterior of an empty building from midnight until 6:00 A.M.). The recommended topics for basic orientation and training include the following:

Prevention/Protection Training

- patrolling
- checking for hazards
- access control
- fire control systems
- alarm systems
- shoplifting prevention techniques
- personnel control
- law enforcement/private security relationships

A knowledge of these topics will help acclimate new security employees to their environment and provide officers with general information that will increase their overall effectiveness.

Enforcement

- surveillance techniques
- techniques and restrictions on searching
- crime scene preservation
- handling juveniles
- handling mentally disturbed people
- dealing with employees
- observation/description
- preservation of evidence
- criminal/civil law
- interviewing techniques
- report writing
- loss prevention techniques
- arrest techniques

General Emergency Services

- accidents and first aid
- defensive tactics
- fire fighting
- communications
- crowd control
- crimes in progress

Special Problems

- escorts
- vandalism
- arson
- burglary
- robbery
- theft
- alcohol/drugs

To be properly covered, these subjects will require 30 to 40 hours of training time. The time allocated for a given subject will vary with circumstances. For example, in a company that has employees trained in first aid on staff the new security officer may only need five minutes of instruction about what to do in the event of an injury incident.

Although 40 hours of instruction may seem like an extraordinary amount of time in view of what many retailers do today, we prefer to think of it as an investment in the future. After all, security personnel are hired to protect people and assets. One cannot protect assets by paying legal fees, settlements, or civil liability awards or by creating public ill will as a result of a security employee's action. After an adverse incident connected with a security agent's conduct, how many retailers wouldn't concede that training would have been a good investment?

On-the-Job Training

There's nothing wrong with on-the-job training (OJT) if it's done properly. Indeed, it can be a very effective way to lead a new employee through the learning process. Unfortunately, too many times the trainer isn't prepared to train, and the instruction lacks direction and definition. More often than not, the OJT isn't documented.

The following are recommendations for an effective OJT program:

1. Those employees who are designated as trainers should be willing and eager to assume that responsibility.
2. Trainers should be recognized as such by title—for example, Senior Detective,

Senior Officer, Trainer—and they should receive a salary incentive for this important duty.

3. Trainers should attend a training session to prepare them for their task.
4. Trainers should have a structured program to lead the trainee through, and they should formally note the completion of each phase of the program.
5. Trainers must formally rate the progress of the trainee, and this rating must be documented.
6. Trainers must certify that new employees have satisfactorily progressed to the point that they can function alone.

At the conclusion of the process, the employee's file should include the trainer's identity, the time devoted to the major categories of the OJT, the ratings, and the certification date.

Telephone Training

One easy method of providing ongoing training utilizes a telephone answering machine. A new training message is recorded on the machine each day or each week, as appropriate. Each security officer must call in and listen to the training message at the required interval. A technique for ensuring that the employee does in fact listen to the message is to ask a question at the end and have the caller record the answer on the machine. This technique provides a means of auditing the training process and assessing the degree to which the training was understood. Employers who use this training technique should ensure that the messages are preserved.

Training Bulletins

Another ongoing training technique is the printed training bulletin, which can be distributed periodically. Some method of testing comprehension, such as a quiz, is desirable.

Roll-Call Training

The traditional police method of roll-call training (discussing a training topic with the officers who gather for briefing before going on shift) is another technique for training, but this method is only effective when a group of security personnel are all in one place at a specific time on a regular schedule. Roll-call training may use lectures, printed material, or audio-visual aids such as films and videotapes. Audio-visual techniques are extremely effective because people remember more when material is both seen and heard than when only one sense is involved.

Subscription Training

Some companies and individuals provide ready-made security training materials that can be obtained through a paid subscription. One example is the *Retail Security Digest,*[4] which not only provides commentary and updates on various security-related news and legal decisions but also includes a monthly lesson. The lesson presents various scenarios in which security personnel frequently find themselves and then poses questions to determine if the reader understands the correct solution. A typical lesson follows:

LESSON FOR THE MONTH*

(Another thrilling episode with I. V. GOTCHYA and KEN KETCHEM)

REVIEW SCENARIO #3

On a busy evening two nights before Christmas at approximately 8:45 P.M., our trusty store detective, I. V. GOTCHYA, stationed himself inconspicuously just inside the main exit doors of a branch mall store of the CHEAP BROTHERS DEPARTMENT STORE CHAIN.

These doors led directly to the parking lot area outside of the CHEAP BROTHERS STORE.

As GOTCHYA stood at his position, he began to observe the customers exiting the store to determine if all of the customers had stapled to their CHEAP BROTHERS paper bags the receipt for their purchase of CHEAP BROTHERS merchandise.

Shortly after taking up his position, GOTCHYA had cause to observe one A. GOODFELLOW, a male approximately twenty-two years of age who was walking through the exit doors carrying two huge CHEAP BROTHERS paper bags, both apparently filled with merchandise and neither displaying any sign of a stapled sales receipt.

As GOODFELLOW walked out into the parking lot, GOTCHYA followed behind him and caught up with him approximately 50 feet from the store.

GOTCHYA approached GOODFELLOW from behind, making no physical contact with GOODFELLOW. GOTCHYA spoke to him, explained who he was, and showed GOODFELLOW his store identification card.

GOTCHYA inquired of GOODFELLOW regarding the merchandise in the bags, and he answered that all of the merchandise was CHEAP BROTHERS merchandise that he and his wife had just purchased.

---

*Source: Courtesy of *Retail Security Digest,* published by the Law Offices of Robert L. Barry, P.C., 222 Middle Country Road, Smithtown, NY 11787, phone 1-800-223-6575.

When GOTCHYA asked for the receipts, GOODFELLOW became very apologetic and explained that his wife, who was still shopping inside the store, saves all sales receipts and that most certainly she had the receipts in her possession inside the store.

GOODFELLOW suggested that the two bags of merchandise, which by this time were getting quite heavy, be brought to GOODFELLOW's car with GOTCHYA and that GOTCHYA would be permitted to inventory all of the merchandise at the car and take the list of purchased merchandise back into the store with GOODFELLOW in search of MRS. GOODFELLOW.

GOTCHYA agreed to GOODFELLOW'S proposal; and after the merchandise was inventoried, they re-entered the crowded store looking for MRS. GOODFELLOW.

After some twenty minutes of looking, GOTCHYA explained that he had to return to his post and suggested that the store page MRS. GOODFELLOW.

MR. GOODFELLOW readily agreed to this; and he, at GOTCHYA'S invitation, walked up the staircase to the security office where GOTCHYA could arrange for MRS. GOODFELLOW to be paged.

No physical contact of any kind was had on GOODFELLOW while en route to the security office.

When they entered the security office, KEN KETCHEM was seated at a desk talking to a uniformed police officer about the upcoming Super Bowl playoffs. There was no one else in the security office at that time.

GOTCHYA explained the facts of this matter so far and explained that he had to return to the first floor of the store.

He invited GOODFELLOW to sit down and asked KETCHEM to have MRS. GOODFELLOW paged and asked to report to the security office. As he left the security office, GOTCHYA turned over to KETCHEM the inventory list of the merchandise that was still in GOODFELLOW'S car.

As soon as GOTCHYA left, the uniformed police officer voluntarily expressed to KETCHEM that he didn't believe GOODFELLOW'S story, whereupon KETCHEM invited the police officer to ask GOODFELLOW some questions and admonished GOODFELLOW that he best not lie to the police.

At this, GOODFELLOW rose in anger and shouted, "I have taken enough of this crap—I'm leaving;" and as he stood up to leave, the police officer grabbed GOODFELLOW by the arm, and, as GOODFELLOW resisted, the officer took out his sap and struck GOODFELLOW on the head dazing GOODFELLOW.

KETCHEM immediately realized that some action was in order, and he immediately handcuffed the hands of the still dazed GOODFELLOW behind his back and told him he was under arrest for assaulting the police officer.

At about this point, MRS. GOODFELLOW, who was pregnant, arrived in the security office to see if they could help her locate her missing husband.

At the sight of her husband lying face down on the floor of the security office, handcuffed and bleeding, MRS. GOODFELLOW fainted and fell to the office floor next to her husband.

Shortly after arriving at the emergency room of the nearby hospital, MRS. GOODFELLOW had a miscarriage and lost the child she was carrying.

Hospital authorities found in her handbag sales receipts for each and every piece of merchandise in the bags that her husband was carrying.

QUIZ

1. GOTCHYA had the right to ask GOODFELLOW about the merchandise in the bags.

   True _____   False _____

2. When GOTCHYA stopped GOODFELLOW in the parking lot, he in fact detained or apprehended him.

   True _____   False _____

3. When GOODFELLOW admitted that all of the merchandise in the bags was CHEAP BROTHERS merchandise, GOTCHYA had reasonable grounds to detain or arrest GOODFELLOW.

   True _____   False _____

4. The searching of the bags and the listing of the merchandise by GOTCHYA was an illegal search since no arrest of GOODFELLOW had been made.

   True _____   False _____

5. When GOODFELLOW went to the security office with GOTCHYA, he in fact was in the state of arrest and in the custody of GOTCHYA.

   True _____   False _____

6. KETCHEM was right in letting the police officer stay in the office since the sight of the uniform may make GOODFELLOW be more truthful.

   True _____   False _____

7. KETCHEM should not have let the police officer question GOODFELLOW in this matter.

   True _____   False _____

8. KETCHEM should have ordered the police officer not to interfere and to leave the office.

   True _____   False _____

9. The police officer had probable cause to arrest GOODFELLOW, especially when he tried to leave the office.

   True _____   False _____

10. KETCHEM made a good arrest of GOODFELLOW for his assault on the police officer.

    True _____   False _____

11. KETCHEM and CHEAP BROTHERS DEPARTMENT STORE are liable to GOODFELLOW for letting the police officer wrongfully assault him.

    True _____   False _____

12. KETCHEM and CHEAP BROTHERS DEPARTMENT STORE are liable for causing the miscarriage of the baby MRS. GOODFELLOW was carrying.

    True _____   False _____

QUIZ MARKING KEY

1. True. GOTCHYA had every right to inquire or to ask GOODFELLOW about the merchandise, and his mere asking in no way infringed upon the rights of GOODFELLOW.

2. False. GOTCHYA made no physical contact with GOODFELLOW or indicated in any way by his words that GOODFELLOW was not free to go. He merely asked GOODFELLOW about the merchandise in the bags. The rest of the actions were volunteered by GOODFELLOW.

3. False. GOODFELLOW, in addition to admitting that the merchandise was CHEAP BROTHERS merchandise, also gave GOTCHYA a reasonable story that it had been paid for and that his wife had the receipts, and he even volunteered to go to get the receipts with GOTCHYA.

4. False. GOTCHYA'S examination of the bags was a consent search, not only freely agreed to by GOODFELLOW but in fact freely volunteered by him. You need no arrest to couple with a consent search.

5. False. Again, there remained no physical contact or any other conduct that GOODFELLOW was forced to go upstairs to the security office. The fact pattern recites that GOODFELLOW was invited upstairs for the purpose of having his wife paged.

6. False. This was KETCHEM'S first, although never his last, mistake. The police officer had no connection whatsoever with the facts in this case at that point. His presence was not necessary and could create the appearance that GOODFELLOW was under arrest. Further, on the outside chance that GOOD-FELLOW may have later given admissions concerning the theft of merchandise, these admissions could later be inadmissible if the Miranda warnings were not given, due to the presence of the police officer in the security office.

7. True. The police officer had no position in even being in the room, much less participating in the questioning of GOODFELLOW.

8. True. Obviously, KETCHEM again dropped the ball in not asking the officer to refrain from participating in the case and telling him to leave when he failed to abide by KETCHEM'S wishes. This was totally and solely a CHEAP BROTHERS DEPARTMENT STORE matter at this point and of no interest or business to the police officer. KETCHEM failed to dominate and control his business.

9. False. Obviously, the police officer had nothing other than a fogged understanding of criminal procedure law and an inflated understanding of his authority.

10. False. The interference by the police officer was illegal. A citizen has the right to resist an unlawful arrest even being made by a police officer, and GOOD-FELLOW'S actions were lawful. KETCHEM not only effected a false arrest of GOODFELLOW but committed an assault as well when he put the handcuffs on GOODFELLOW.

11. True. Absolutely liable in negligence for permitting the police officer to commit such wrongs against GOODFELLOW while on CHEAP BROTHERS property and in the presence of one of their security personnel.

12. This question has no clear definitive answer. Generally, most jurisdictions under present law would not permit recovery since no one committed any act overt or passive toward MRS. GOODFELLOW. Certainly, at a minimum,

however, these circumstances would be considered by a jury when awarding damages to MR. GOODFELLOW. At a maximum, the fact pattern of this kind of case influences and impacts a court to create new law and permit recovery of damages by MRS. GOODFELLOW for the atrocious conduct of KETCHEM.

Interactive Video Training

A new technique for training security personnel is interactive video, which utilizes a computer-based video disc and associated equipment. Interactive video training presents various security scenarios and allows the viewer to answer questions throughout the presentation by touching "answer blocks" on the video screen. For example, during scenarios of typical shoplifting techniques and suspect responses, the presentation will stop at appropriate times to pose questions to the viewer. Such questions as "At this point, you should (a) stop the suspect, (b) continue to watch the suspect, (c) call your supervisor, or (d) discontinue your surveillance and resume your patrol" are typical of those asked to test whether the student knows when a suspected shoplifter should be approached. After the viewer touches the appropriate answer block on the video screen, the video either accepts the correct choice and proceeds with the scenario or indicates that the answer was incorrect and automatically goes back and reviews the subject. This review gives the student a second chance to choose the correct answer.

These systems also keep a record of the student's choices and print it at the end of the session for the trainer. These records may indicate such traits as over-aggressiveness, indecisiveness, and other characteristics that might adversely affect future performance.

The equipment required for this very sophisticated and realistic training is not inexpensive. However, if large numbers of people require training, the equipment is cost effective because students are trained without supervision except for a brief initial introduction to the technique and a review of the results. A full day is normally required to complete a training session.

Seminars and Workshop Training

One of the many values of seminars and workshops is what is called *group dynamics,* that is, peers gathered together focusing on a common topic and exchanging experiences in connection with it. If the workshop focuses on courtroom testimony and demeanor, for example, participants will share both good and bad experiences. This sharing can be meaningful and beneficial, and it will occur in addition to the facilitator's instructional information about the topic.

A wealth of talent is available for presentations; an outside consultant, attorney, or other kind of specialist can enhance and professionalize the program.

Seminars and workshops can be held in-house, or they can be a collective effort of numerous retailers. Stores Protective Association of Los Angeles has for years offered short training programs to the advantage of many retailers in the western United States.

TRAINING RECORDS

It is essential that all training given to security personnel be thoroughly documented and that these records be retained throughout the employee's tenure.

A caution is in order with respect to files. We urge that a separate training file be maintained, and that only notations with respect to training be included. All other personnel data should be kept in the employee's personnel file. Should a lawsuit be filed alleging any type of negligence action, it may be possible to produce the employee's training file without producing the entire personnel file. The latter may contain data that your attorney would prefer be kept confidential.

TESTS

In addition to preserving a written record of all training given, trainees should be required to take some type of test to prove that they absorbed and understood the training they received. Although providing training is essential, it is equally important that the employee understands the training. A simple written test, either true-false or fill-in-the-blank, will satisfy this requirement, provided that records of the tests and the results are maintained and that the tests were honestly given and passed. So-called guaranteed-to-pass tests have limited value and may actually be a disadvantage if it can be shown that the training given was superficial and for appearances only.

The following are sample questions that can be used to test the comprehension and understanding of students who have received training in shoplifting activities. Ideally, the training will be presented in absorbable segments, and the appropriate questions used at the end of each segment. The answers are enclosed in square brackets ([ ]).

True/False Questions

1. When you are involved in apprehending a shoplifter who has stolen small items such as gloves, wallets, or jewelry, special care must be exercised. [T]
2. You can keep anything that is the personal property of the shoplifter and hold it indefinitely in the security office. [F]
3. It's permissible to make a shoplifting apprehension on the word of a selling employee if that employee is a good friend and trustworthy. [F]

Multiple-Choice Questions

1. You approach a customer in the belief that he has stolen merchandise from the store, but you quickly realize that a mistake has been made. You should:
    a. Minimize the damage by apologizing and allowing the person to leave immediately.
    b. Attempt to obtain a release in the security office.
    c. Write a report but notify your supervisor only if a complaint is later filed.
    d. Identify yourself as a security officer and leave immediately.
    [Answer: A]
2. A shoplifter is running out of the store with a large quantity of merchandise. She gets into a car standing in front of the store and starts to drive away. You should:
    a. Get into your car and chase her as she drives away.
    b. Take the license number and call the police.
    c. Send a salesperson to chase her while you call the police.
    d. Try to reach in the car to obtain the ignition keys.
    [Answer: B]

Fill-In Questions

1. Methods for working the floor vary with each security representative. Some can easily spot a shoplifter, while others, no matter how determined, cannot "see" what they are looking at. After spotting a shoplifter, you must not let him or her out of your sight. The requirements that must be met before a shoplifter can be apprehended are
    a. [Know] the merchandise belongs to your store.
    b. [See] the suspect take the merchandise.
    c. [Know] where the merchandise is located.
    d. [Know] that the merchandise is still in the possession of the suspect.
2. The intent of the shoplifter to steal must be proven in order to obtain a criminal conviction. Some of the more obvious acts that can show criminal intent are:
    1. [Concealing the merchandise.]
    2. [Removing and discarding price tickets.]
    3. [Removing merchandise from the selling area and passing by cash registers without making any attempt to pay.]

SUMMARY

Employers have an obligation to provide their employees with the tools and training they need to do their assigned jobs properly; employees have the obligation to

AGENT TRAINING REPORT

INSTRUCTIONS: To fill in the type of training field, please use the number that corresponds to the appropriate training.

1. Basic agent training
2. Advanced agent training
3. Legal seminar
4. Lesson of the month (reviews)
5. Management seminar
6. Self-defense seminar
7. Junior executive development
8. Communications seminar
9. In-store training
10. Interview/interrogation seminar
11. Other (use explanation column to specify)

Dates are to be listed as follows: One day of training on June 6th, 1991, would be shown by putting 6-1-91 under both the FROM and TO columns under FIRST WEEK of the DATES OF TRAINING section. More than one day would be indicated by placing the dates under the same FROM and TO columns under the FIRST WEEK section. If the training goes into two weeks, use both the FIRST WEEK and SECOND WEEK FROM and TO columns.

EXPLANATION column should be used to elaborate on training. If you select number 5 (for TYPE OF TRAINING) you might put "How to delegate assignments" in the EXPLANATION column.

If no TEST SCORE is available, leave the space blank. If you have a test score, list it as _____ out of _____.

AGENT NUMBER: _____ AGENT NAME: _____

DATES OF TRAINING				TOTAL HOURS	TYPE OF TRAINING (use #)	EXPLANATION	TEST SCORE
FIRST WEEK		SECOND WEEK					
FROM	TO	FROM	TO				

Figure 5–3 Agent training report.

SECURITY TRAINING RECORD

SECURITY AGENT _____

EMPLOYEE NUMBER _____

DATE OF HIRE _____

DATE	SUBJECT	TIME SPENT	TRAINER

Figure 5–4   Security training record.

understand the rules governing their employment and to abide by them. Training enables employers and employees to meet their mutual obligations.

The security employees' job is unique in many respects. Their job functions place them in a special position; they have the authority to detain, interrogate, and arrest people. The opportunities for abusing these powers are numerous. When abuses do occur, they subject the employee and the employer to legal liability and potential damage awards, which can amount to millions of dollars.[5] If the court finds that the employers did not meet their reasonable duty to minimize abuses through the proper screening, selection, training, supervision, and management of their employees, then the employers may be found negligent. This finding carries with it the potential for severe civil damages.[6]

When discussing the importance of the proper selection and training of security personnel, we often say that new entry-level security officers walk around with a blank check in their pocket, signed by their employer. Whether that check is ever deposited, by whom, and for how much, may depend on the diligence and care with which the security officer was selected and trained and the meticulousness with which records evidencing that diligence and care were maintained.

There are many excellent sources[7] for information on training content and methods; the following things must be kept in mind:

- Training must be relevant to the job assignment.
- Training must be thorough.
- Training must be ongoing.
- The trainee must be tested to ensure comprehension.
- Records of training and testing must be maintained. For examples of training records, see Figures 5–3 and 5–4.

NOTES

1. Charles P. Nemeth, *Private Security and the Law* (Cincinnati: Anderson Publishing Co., 1989).
2. Charles A. Sennewald, *Effective Security Management,* 2nd ed. (Stoneham, Mass.: Butterworths, 1985).
3. See note 3 *supra,* Chapter 2.
4. The *Retail Security Digest* is published monthly by the Law Offices of Robert L. Barry, P.C., 222 Middle Country Road, Smithtown, NY 11787, phone 1-800-223-6575.
5. In Geringer v. Zayre Corp., 1989, a Florida couple was awarded $2.25 million in damages as a result of a shoplifting arrest. The case was reported in *Security Law Newsletter,* vol. 9, no. 4 (April 1989), p. 42. Published by Crime Control Research Corporation, Washington, DC 20007.
6. In Globe Security Systems v. Sterling, 1989, $500,000 in punitive damages was reversed on appeal. The *Security Law Newsletter* notes that "training and manuals can defend against punitive awards."
7. For example, Walter M. Strobl, *Handbook for Industrial/Commercial Security Forces— Training Guide* (Memphis: Strobl Security Service, 1977). Distributed by Training Consultants, Inc., PO Box 81, Knoxville, TN 37901; Ronald R. Minion, ed., *The Protection Officer Training Manual* (Cochrane, Alberta, Canada: Protection Officer Publications, 1986). See also organizations such as the American Society for Industrial Security, 1655 North Fort Myer Drive, Suite 1200, Arlington, VA 22209.

6

Policies and Procedures for Handling Shoplifters

It is essential to establish policies and procedures for handling shoplifters for very important legal and business reasons. Policies and procedures establish the firm's operating guidelines. Absent such guidelines, uniformity and consistency of action and performance are not ensured. Surely there is no facet of business in which uniformity and consistency are more important. In this chapter we discuss

- authority to apprehend
- probable cause to detain
- use of force
- disposition of the shoplifter
- documenting the event

AUTHORITY TO APPREHEND

Which employees should have the authority to detain, apprehend, and prosecute shoplifters? This is a vital question because the answer determines the extent to which the business owner will place his legal and financial exposure to liability in the hands of others. At the risk of redundancy, we constantly stress the potential civil and criminal liability inherent in dealing with shoplifters; merchants accept this risk because of the seriousness and pervasiveness of shoplifting. When authorizing an employee to detain shoplifters, the merchant delegates to this employee a major responsibility. The merchants likewise have a major responsibility: They must determine and promulgate the policies and procedures under which the authority to apprehend is to be exercised. Only when the merchant establishes these guidelines and the employees delegated this authority understand their responsibilities have both parties met their minimum legal and ethical obligations.

Who, then, should be given the authority to detain shoplifters? There is no definitive answer to this question, but there are several factors that should be considered in arriving at an answer. First, the business owner should consider granting apprehension authority to a limited number of employees; this limits potential liability. The number of people selected for this authority must be sufficient to respond adequately to shoplifting problems during all of the hours that the store is open.

Second, the mental and emotional maturity of the employee should be a major factor in this decision. The people selected to make shoplifting apprehensions must be those who will remain calm in stressful situations. Employees who lose control at the slightest provocation are not the ones who should be dealing with shoplifters. Obviously, common sense and good judgment must be mandatory qualities of those entrusted to confront shoplifters.

Most businesses do not enjoy the luxury of having designated security professionals whose only function is to deal with loss prevention and shoplifting problems. In most businesses, regular employees are the ones who deal with shoplifters. This does not mean, however, that the guidelines set forth in the previous chapters regarding the selection and training of security personnel cannot be adapted and applied, to some degree at least, in the selection of the regular employees who will be authorized to detain shoplifters. Thus, business owners should select those employees who meet the criteria set forth in the previous chapters and ensure that they receive the training necessary to deal properly and effectively with shoplifters. This will minimize any negligent training claims against management. It may be true that an employee who deals with a shoplifter may be held to a somewhat lesser standard of care than a professional security officer, but this will not excuse the mishandling of a shoplifting incident.

The minimum shoplifting detection training required for nonsecurity employees includes a clear understanding of the six steps required before a detention can be made:

1. You must see the suspect approach the merchandise.
2. You must see the suspect take possession of the merchandise.
3. You must see where the suspect conceals it.
4. You must maintain an uninterrupted surveillance to ensure that the suspect doesn't dispose of the merchandise.
5. You must see the suspect fail to pay for the merchandise.
6. You should approach the suspect outside.

Additionally, nonsecurity employees who are specifically authorized to make detentions should be instructed to avoid any physical force other than an initial holding force (if necessary). If violence erupts or escalates, they should allow the shoplifter to escape rather than risk injury to the employee, to bystanders, or to the thief.

Employees who are not authorized to make detentions should be instructed and encouraged to approach customers they believe or suspect have committed a theft, greet them, offer assistance, and generally convey the message that they are aware of them. Such "good customer service" tends to deter shoplifting or completion of the act, and makes all employees partners in the store's defense against losses caused by shoplifters.

PROBABLE CAUSE TO DETAIN

Probable cause is sometimes called *reasonable cause*, although in some jurisdictions the two terms have different legal meanings. Probable cause is a very complicated legal concept that has been the subject of dozens of appellate court decisions and a topic of continuing legal dispute. When does probable cause exist and make the detention of a shoplifter legally justified? Considering the complexity of this legal concept, how can we expect the average sales associate or security officer to deal effectively with it? The simple answer is that most businesses should avoid this complication by establishing detention policies and procedures that do not require the application or involvement of probable cause.

The laws of most jurisdictions require that a misdemeanor (the degree of criminal offense severity under which shoplifting usually falls) be committed in the presence of a private citizen before that citizen can arrest an offender for the crime. (See Chapter 8 for a full discussion of the legal aspects of shoplifting.) This fact notwithstanding, some states have enacted "merchant privilege" statutes that permit retailers who suspect a customer of shoplifting to detain that customer if such suspicion rises to the level of the legal definition and standard of probable cause. Other states rely on case law, as opposed to statutory law, which allows the merchant to stop a customer for a reasonable inquiry.

It is this aspect of the law (that is, the merchants' privilege and the probable cause basis for detaining a shoplifter) that creates many of the legal problems connected with shoplifting detentions. When does the sales associate's mere suspicion rise to the level of legal probable cause? This is a legal question that is generally answered by a court. It is for this reason that we recommend that employees, security professionals, and nonprofessionals be instructed and cautioned not to detain a customer based on probable cause even if the law permits. Employees should be required to witness the theft before detaining the suspect. This approach is legally sound and the best form of litigation prevention. For all but a very few exceptional situations (which will be discussed in Chapter 8), we suggest that before any customer is detained and questioned about shoplifting, the employee making the detention *must* have seen the customer take an item of merchandise and attempt to leave the store without paying for it. This approach is easily understood by the employee, it is legally sound, and it is enforceable by management; it leaves little room for interpretation or imagination.

USE OF FORCE

What should merchants instruct their employees with respect to the use of force in detaining and apprehending suspects? Obviously, the first consideration should be to follow the law of the jurisdiction concerned. Competent legal counsel should be sought in this regard. Generally, the employee or security officer is permitted to use only non-deadly force in dealing with shoplifters. The amount of non-deadly force permitted is strictly limited to *only* that amount of force required to just overcome the force used by the shoplifter for the protection of the person making the detention. Some jurisdictions permit the use of non-deadly force to prevent the escape of the shoplifter or the loss of the stolen merchandise (evidence), but this extension of the permissible use of force is not universal. The use of force is one of the most litigated aspects of the shoplifter detention and apprehension process.

The policy on use of force you select will not only depend on applicable laws but also on your concerns about your public image. Although the law may permit the use of reasonable (necessary) force to prevent the escape of the shoplifter, do you want the public image that results from customers observing your employees wrestling another "customer" to the ground? Do you want your employees chasing a shoplifter through the mall or the parking lot? Will your answer to this last question depend on whether the shoplifter has dropped the stolen merchandise or still has it? How far do you want your employees to pursue a fleeing shoplifter? While some of these questions go beyond the issue of force, they require a decision on your part and must be incorporated into your policies and procedures.

The use of handcuffs is another subject about which there are varying opinions. Should security personnel carry handcuffs, and if so, what rules should govern their use?

The use of handcuffs by employees who are not dedicated security personnel properly trained in their use should be prohibited. Handcuffs, improperly applied or used, can cause serious injury. Therefore, anyone using handcuffs must be trained in their proper use.

Assuming that the security agent has been trained in the proper use of handcuffs and carries them while on duty, when should they be used? To answer this question, we must keep in mind why handcuffs are used: They are devices to help control and restrict the use of a person's hands and arms, and they are properly used to help ensure the safety of the arresting officer, the suspect, or both. The term *arresting officer* is used purposefully; regardless of the intention of the security officer, whenever handcuffs are applied to a shoplifter, that person has been arrested.

When should handcuffs be used? Obviously, only if the suspect is to be arrested and only if such use is really necessary. For example, when a 15-year-old female shoplifter who is slight of build and has not shown any indication to fight or flee is arrested, the use of handcuffs is probably not necessary. Similarly, if an elderly suspect has been arrested and is now in the store security office being processed before the arrival of the police, it is probably not necessary to handcuff this person.

The subject of handcuffing is controversial. Even the authors have differences of opinion as to when handcuffs should be used. In some cases the need for their use will be quite obvious; in other cases it will be a judgment call. In either situation, handcuffs must be properly applied and their use must be justifiable and reasonable under the circumstances.

The issue of the use of force is clearly one that demonstrates the necessity of choosing the right personnel for making shoplifting apprehensions. The good judgment of the employee in these situations is critical, and mature and level headed decisions are essential. While the use of excessive force cannot be tolerated, neither can management, after giving an employee the responsibility of protecting their assets and the authority to detain shoplifters, deny that employee the right to adequately and legally defend himself if attacked while performing his assigned duties.

The issue of the security employee's right to use force for self-defense is clear. More often than not, however, the issue of force doesn't focus on defensive force but rather on offensive force used by employees to overcome the shoplifter's resistance or efforts to escape detention. If in a struggle the shoplifter's finger is broken, the theft is overshadowed by the excessive force used by the security agent.

With regards to pursuing a shoplifter, if the shoplifter or employee knocks down a customer or passer-by, the resultant injury may drive a civil action against the store.

The bottom line is that each retail store must determine its own policy and then develop guidelines for employees to follow. It's a balancing act because of the endless number of possible scenarios. If the retailer allows security agents to use force, then those agents must understand the importance of using sound judgment as to how far to go and when to back off and let the culprit get away. Perhaps that is the very crux of the matter: Security employee's pride and sense of self-esteem tend to be at stake, and to lose a shoplifter is embarrassing. Retailers should create a climate in which it's permissible to "lose" a shoplifter. It's certainly far better to have 100 shoplifters get away than to have anyone injured. After all, what's the value of the lost merchandise compared to the possible pain and suffering of those injured and potential financial loss caused by a lawsuit?

DISPOSITION OF THE SHOPLIFTER

Once a person has been detained for the theft of merchandise, the store owner must decide what to do with that individual. There are three options:

1. warn and release
2. conditional release
3. prosecution

Warn and Release

Should shoplifters be given a warning? Should first-time offenders be treated differently than repeat offenders? What form should a warning take? Is a warning the equivalent of an accusation? Should the warning be verbal or written? Should it be acknowledged in writing and signed by the shoplifter? These are all questions that the business owner or manager must resolve; the answers must be incorporated into the store's policies and procedures.

In general, warning shoplifters is not a good idea. If all the requirements have been met to warrant a detention and if the shoplifter has the stolen merchandise in possession, then the shoplifter should be arrested. Arrest does not necessarily mean criminal prosecution through the courts; the store owner or employee may choose to release the shoplifter before calling the police and initiating formal prosecution.

Chapter 14 discusses the subtle distinctions between these various terms or actions, but at this point suffice it to say that whenever a shoplifter is detained, it is probably the legal equivalent of an arrest. Prosecution, which moves shoplifters into the criminal justice system and subjects them to a criminal record and trial, is a separate step that does not automatically follow a detention or arrest.

To detain shoplifters and then simply advise them that they should not shoplift again seems counterproductive. If being caught in the act of shoplifting is to be at all meaningful to them and act as a deterrent to such behavior in the future, it seems that simply being scolded by an employee is insufficient.

Conditional Release

The conditional release, sometimes referred to as a *controlled release*, occurs when detainees are released without formal prosecution but are warned that if caught again, they will be formally prosecuted for the second offense as well as for the first. Some limitations exist on the permissible time that may elapse between the offenses. The conditional release procedure is recommended over the first option where legally allowed.

Another reason we suggest something more than simply a scolding is that, all things being equal, the legal liabilities are similar whenever you detain a shoplifter, regardless of whether you warn, arrest and conditionally release, or arrest and prosecute him or her. Because this is the case, you might as well get the most deterrent value you can out of the detention.

Prosecution

Should shoplifters be prosecuted? This question is best answered by reviewing all the pertinent aspects affecting this decision.

The first consideration is the practical business matter of whether the owner can afford to have employees spend time in court testifying. This consideration will obviously be conditioned by several factors: the number of shoplifting arrests made each month, the average number of such cases that actually go to trial (as opposed to being decided before trial by a plea bargain or guilty plea), and finally the policies of the local prosecuting or district attorney.

If a business makes only one or two shoplifting arrests each month, then the time involved in having employees go to court to testify in these cases will likely be minimal. If, on the other hand, the business is a large department store that employs a large security staff, it would not be unusual for more than 50 arrests a month to occur. In this case, the number of arrests may be a factor in determining prosecution policies. For example, the owner may decide that only the more egregious cases will actually be prosecuted, setting a dollar limit under which the shoplifter will be given a conditional release.

In our experience, most shoplifting cases never require a trial.* The majority of shoplifting prosecutions are resolved by guilty pleas or, in the case of repeat offenders, plea bargains. These resolutions rarely require the arresting employee to testify, and therefore time spent in court is usually not a major consideration.

The policies of the local prosecuting attorney also must be considered when setting your prosecution policy. For example, the local prosecutor may have a policy of dismissing misdemeanor charges for shoplifting merchandise with a value below a certain dollar amount. Such policies often arise due to crowded court calendars and other more serious crime problems that take priority over shoplifting. If the prosecutor has such a policy, it is a waste of time to call the local police and have a shoplifting suspect charged only to have the prosecutor eventually dismiss the case. In any event, it is important to contact the local prosecuting authority to discuss the current prosecution policy so that your decisions will take these issues into account.

One of the main reasons given for adopting a policy of always prosecuting shoplifters is that prosecution is thought to act as a deterrent to others. The often ignored part of this rationale is that for prosecution to act as a deterrent to others, the others must know of the policy. In small towns, for example, where the local newspaper prints a column dedicated to police activities, which lists all the local citizens who have been arrested during the past week, an arrest and prosecution policy may very well be appropriate. In large cities, however, where the arrest and prosecution of a shoplifter is never publicized, prosecution may not achieve the desired deterrent result.

---

*In our experience, fewer than 10% of all prosecutions require the arresting security officer to appear in court. However, this low percentage may be skewed because the arrests are made by professional security personnel; stores that use sales associates for shoplifting apprehensions may experience more court trials because the employees' inexperience may result in more procedural errors or other reasons for shoplifters to feel they will prevail if the case goes before a jury.

In some communities, a store's reputation for being tough on shoplifters may be transmitted by people who are "street smart," and some school-age youngsters may pass the word among their peers. However, many shoplifters aren't in the schoolyard or street-smart communication loop, and they don't know what a given store's position is. If caught, they surely won't share such information over bridge or at a lodge meeting, so a tough pro-prosecution policy is lost on this segment of the community.

Whenever there is evidence that the shoplifter is a professional, prosecution should always occur. The word that you prosecute will be circulated among professional shoplifters, who tend to work businesses that don't prosecute. After all, why steal from a store where you'll be prosecuted if you're caught, when it's just as easy to steal from a store that doesn't prosecute?

Similarly, if a shoplifter who was given a conditional release is apprehended again, it is essential that he or she be prosecuted for both the present and the former offense. After all, shoplifters who were released with a warning were advised that this would happen, and if they see fit to steal from you again, they should be subjected to all the available remedies and penalties, including prosecution.

Finally, the issue of prosecution is a philosophical one. Some business owners prefer to deal more forgivingly with shoplifters and forego prosecution in exchange for the shoplifter's promise not to steal again. Some business owners simply have an aversion to getting involved with the criminal justice system. Conversely, other owners take a very aggressive attitude toward shoplifting, and they wouldn't think of not prosecuting a shoplifter.

If the decision on whether to prosecute is not clearly dictated by business or other considerations, then prosecution is the best policy.

After a person has been arrested for shoplifting and charged, it is not unusual that the store owner will get a call from the shoplifter, his attorney, his religious advisor, or his physician or psychiatrist seeking to convince the store owner that the act of shoplifting was completely out of character for the shoplifter, or that the shoplifter succumbed to some uncontrollable urge because of a medical, psychiatric, or personal problem. The caller will ask the store owner to reconsider her position and withdraw prosecution "in the interests of justice." *Do not* acquiesce to these requests. In the first place, once the case is referred to the prosecuting attorney, the store owner loses control of the prosecution process; it is now in the control of the prosecutor. Moreover, there are established procedures by which such cases can be civilly compromised through the courts. We do not suggest this practice. After all, once you start the wheels of justice turning, you engage the efforts of many people, and it is rarely justifiable to stop the process and render worthless all the effort that has gone into the prosecution.

There is another reason for not withdrawing prosecution: Shoplifters commit a crime, and any determination as to their eventual punishment should be made by a jury of their peers and not the victim. Additionally, once you begin yielding to these requests, you can no longer in good conscience choose which you will yield to and which you will refuse. The best policy to follow is to state simply to all callers that your policy is that once an arrest is made and referred to the prosecutor, the matter is then totally out of your hands. The caller should be referred to the prosecutor and told that if sufficient cause exists to dismiss the charges, the prosecutor will handle the matter in accordance with established legal procedures. When this policy is followed, you honestly tell every caller that you have never asked the prosecutor to dismiss any charges. The prosecutor will occasionally call you after receiving such a call and ask you if you really want the charges dismissed (the callers often misrepresent your position and claim you asked them to call to arrange for a dismissal of the charges). The best answer is: "I am not asking for a dismissal; if you feel a dismissal is in the best interests of justice I won't oppose it. If you do decide to dismiss the charges, I'd appreciate a stipulation in the record that we had probable cause to arrest." This latter request will help protect you from a civil suit if the charges are dismissed and the shoplifter later tries to sue you.

DOCUMENTING THE EVENT

A written record of a shoplifting detention should be prepared and kept regardless of whether the shoplifter was prosecuted or not. (See Chapter 9 for a sample apprehension report format.) In most jurisdictions, a person has at least one year from the date of the incident in which to file a lawsuit. Today, with crowded court calendars, it is not unusual for a civil suit over a shoplifting detention to come to trial three or more years after the incident. Written records are vital in such cases to refresh the memories of those involved.

Additionally, if a shoplifter is prosecuted, the responding police agency will require a written report of the incident to process the arrest. These reports must be as detailed as possible and scrupulously accurate; a shoplifting arrest report is an inappropriate place for creative writing.

Reports should be routinely reviewed by management as an auditing and quality control technique to ensure that the policies and procedures for shoplifting detentions and prosecutions are being followed. The reviewer should sign or initial and date the document.

SUMMARY

Policies and procedures regarding such critical issues as who has the authority to make detentions, probable cause to detain, the use of force in detaining a suspected shoplifter, the use of handcuffs, disposing of a detainee, and documenting the incident must be carefully developed and issued in writing.

The so-called false arrests and imprisonment and the excessive use of force are common causes of action in litigation involving retailers. Some tough choices in these areas must be made by management. Too often suspected shoplifters, retail employees, and even innocent bystanders are injured as a result of the questionable use of force in attempting to detain a shoplifter. The better course of action would have been to let the thief flee. To make these decisions, employees need practical guidelines to follow in the form of company policies and procedures.

Practical policies and procedures are also needed regarding the ultimate disposition of a person in custody.

Perhaps in no other area is the need for written policies and procedures more important than in the issues covered in this chapter. Employees cannot be expected to perform effectively and consistently without written guidelines.

7

Prevention and Deterrence Strategies

Although theft occurs in virtually all locations within a retail facility—offices, receiving dock, employee locker rooms—the shoplifter is limited to three areas:

- selling floors
- fitting rooms
- stockrooms

This chapter focuses on these areas of the store. Within these areas, four types of deterrence affect shoplifting:

- standards and procedures
- psychological factors
- design and layout
- equipment

Be forewarned: There is some redundancy because the psychological factor of discouraging theft on the selling floor, for example, also applies in some measure in fitting rooms. However, we're obliged to discuss the prevention and deterrence strategies fully under each area to ensure that the reader appreciates their value.

SELLING FLOORS
Standards and Procedures
Customer Service

Rendering good customer service is a major objective of every retail establishment; it is also the simplest, easiest, and one of the most effective deterrents to shoplifting.

An employee who recognizes and acknowledges a customer, by making eye contact and if possible offering a greeting, does more to deter that person from shoplifting than many of the more costly and sophisticated techniques and equipment designed for this purpose. A sales associate who follows this technique not only deters theft but also sets the stage for a sale. If immediate personal service cannot be given, a visual acknowledgment serves nearly as well. The important factor in acknowledging customers, aside from the benefits of good customer service, is that it lets customers know that someone knows they are there, knows what they look like, and is paying at least a modicum of attention to them.

Unfortunately, many drug, grocery, and other front-end stores fail to capitalize on this technique, and employees who restock and price merchandise and attend to other tasks in the aisles ignore customers. Simply stated, it's an opportunity lost.

Many shoplifters steal because they have little fear of detection or apprehension; the knowledge that their presence has been noted greatly enhances their belief that if they steal they will be detected.

Merchandise Presentation

To prevent tempting the potential shoplifter, some thought should be given to how small, expensive, or desirable merchandise is displayed or presented. For example, are small, costly pieces of jewelry openly displayed on countertops near an exit? Are expensive silk dresses, cameras, or watches displayed in a remote corner where observation by employees is infrequent? If sales counters are arranged in an island configuration, is the center of the island too high to permit sales associates to see a customer on the opposite side of the island? Do high gondolas block the view of expensive merchandise? Some rational thinking must go into the planning of the display of highly pilferable merchandise to protect it from theft.

Reversing Hangers

In this simple procedure, the hooks of garment hangers are alternately placed in the opposite direction on the fixture rod (Figure 7–1). This technique is highly effective in thwarting grab-and-run thefts in which the shoplifter simply grabs an armful of clothing from a fixture and runs out a nearby exit and usually into a waiting car.

Award Programs

A program that rewards sales associates for alertness to shoplifting can pay handsome dividends. Some merchants pay employees who report customers they believe have attempted or are attempting to shoplift, provided that the suspect is subsequently legally apprehended and the stolen merchandise is recovered (Figure 7–2). These programs encourage sales associates to be alert to the shoplifting problem. Many companies establish minimum dollar awards from $5 to $50 for simply reporting a shoplifter who is subsequently apprehended.

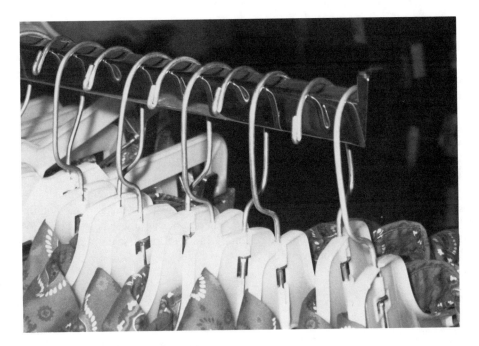

Figure 7–1   Reversing hangers.

loss prevention incentive award program

The Loss Prevention Incentive Award Program provides employees of   with an opportunity to share in substantial awards (see Award Formula on reverse side) and at the same time help reduce our inventory shortages.

awards 50.00 to 1000.00

award formula

Shoplifters	Credit Cards	Internal Dishonesty
10% of the retail value of merchandise recovered with a minimum award of 50.00 and a maximum award of 1000.00.	10% of the retail value of merchandise recovered with a minimum award of 50.00 and a maximum award of 1000.00	10% of recovered merchandise value, or 10% of money recovered, with a minimum award of 200.00 and a maximum award of 1000.00.

Figure 7–2   Loss prevention incentive award program.

Awareness

Employee awareness of the shoplifting problem is a major factor in minimizing shop-lifting losses. Award programs are one method of increasing and rewarding employee awareness. Other things can be done to further heighten awareness; the two methods mentioned here are only designed to stimulate your imagination.

The use of missing merchandise reports, through which employees document every known or suspected loss of merchandise to shoplifting, provide management with an ongoing inventory of the extent of the problem. The execution of these forms by employees is also a means of calling their attention to the problem.

Most employees are unaware of the actual amount of inventory lost to shoplifting. Even when informed of the actual financial loss in their departments, most sales associates do not fully comprehend the true extent of the problem. One method that has proven effective in increasing employee understanding of just how much is lost to shoplifters is to display goods representing the total retail value of merchandise being stolen every hour or every day.

Psychological Factors
Signs

Depending on the nature of the business, signs may be an appropriate shoplifting deterrent. For example, the use of small shelf-edge signs (not unlike shelf-edge price signs) may be useful in grocery markets and drug stores (Figure 7–3). Simple language, such as "Shoplifting is a crime—We prosecute all offenders," is often all that is required. In other cases, and this applies to clothing stores as well, a sign stating "This area is under closed-circuit television surveillance" may be appropriate. Whether the area is actually under constant observation is quite often immaterial. Heed this proviso, however: Signage must not be dishonest. If the store does not have CCTV or the ability to monitor that area with CCTV, then avoid that specific language and say instead, "This area is monitored by security." The sign is intended

Figure 7–3 Shoplifting prevention sign.

only to give the potential shoplifter pause. Remember that most amateur shoplifters steal because they think they will not get caught.

Visible Security Personnel

The use of visible security officers (VSOs) is a very powerful shoplifting deterrent. We equate the effects of using VSOs to the drivers who slow down when they see a highway patrol car parked along the roadside. Visible security officers have the same effect; the potential shoplifter sees the VSO and thinks, "I'd better not shoplift, because if I do, I may get caught."

Neatness of Displays

How goods are displayed and the neatness of presentation can deter shoplifting. The next time you visit a well-run liquor store or grocery market, look at the shelves. Well-run stores of this type invariably have all of the liquor bottles "faced," which means that each bottle is placed near the outer edge of the shelf. This arrangement not only makes for a pleasing visual display but it also makes it very easy for the owner to spot quickly voids where merchandise is missing. The owner (or salesperson or checkout clerk) can normally remember if the "missing" item was sold. If it wasn't, then it was probably shoplifted, and attention can now be given to this area or this merchandise. Most shoplifters are hesitant to steal from neat or patterned displays because the evidence of their theft is more easily noticed, and detection is more likely.

Design and Layout
Openness

As previously stated, shoplifters steal because they think they will not be detected. There is therefore no better way to provide potential shoplifters with a sense of security and anonymity than to design a selling floor full of nooks in which shoplifters are hidden from view. As a general rule, the more open the selling floor, the greater the deterrent to shoplifting. Things that block views—such as walls, high displays, and high selling fixtures—should be avoided if possible.

Register Areas

The proper placement of cash registers is an extremely important shoplifting deterrent. Cash registers are a magnet that attracts employees. They spend an inordinate amount of their time, both productively and otherwise, around the registers. If possible, registers should be placed to provide a strategic view of the selling floor so that the associates can easily see the floor and its merchandise. Items that are shoplifted most frequently should be placed as close to the registers as possible.

Figure 7–4 Security observation booths.

Security Observation Booths

Depending on the design of the store and the professionalism of the shoplifter, it is often important to have a hidden location from which store or security personnel can observe the selling floor. These locations are known by various names, such as *coops* and *Trojan horses*, but they are simply observation or surveillance booths. They can be as simple as a window (preferably a two-way mirror) in a stockroom door or wall facing the selling floor (Figure 7–4) or a heating vent in a wall separating the floor from a stockroom (Figure 7–5) or as complicated as a sophisticated on-floor booth with a cleverly concealed entrance door and 360° vision, which is equipped with a pair of binoculars, a telephone, and CCTV equipment. In some situations, particularly when dealing with professional shoplifters, there is no adequate substitute for a strategically placed booth. In fact, some stores have found that simply placing heating vents or small (12″ × 18″) mirrors on walls without even cutting holes for viewing from the other side is an effective shoplifting deterrent; the potential thief recognizes such devices, is not sure whether they are real or not, and thus is reluctant to shoplift in view of such devices.

Figure 7–5 Heating vent.

Equipment
Mirrors

As discussed, two-way mirrors can be used for observation from booths or stockrooms. Another type of security mirror is the convex mirror (Figure 7–6). This mirror generally ranges in size from 12″ to 36″ in diameter, and it is mounted to provide a generally broad or expansive view of a selling floor area. Normally, these

Figure 7–6 Convex mirror.

mirrors are placed to provide employees at a given location, such as a cash wrap or cash register station, with views of corners and aisleways.

Cables

The use of mechanical and electronic cables to secure merchandise to display fixtures is increasing in popularity (Figures 7–7 and 7–8). Mechanical cable is nothing more than a small diameter (1/8″ to 3/8″) steel airplane cable covered with a plastic sheath,

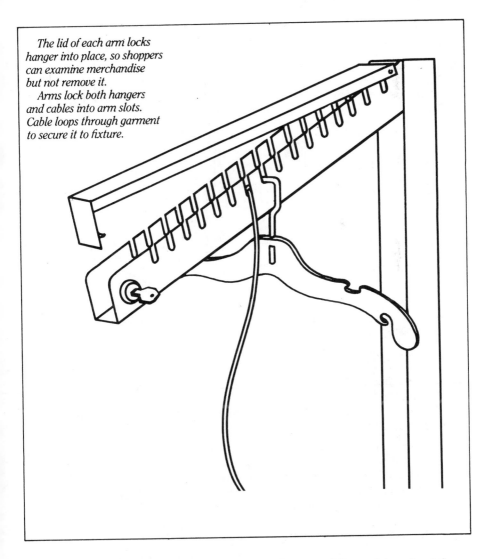

The lid of each arm locks hanger into place, so shoppers can examine merchandise but not remove it.

Arms lock both hangers and cables into arm slots. Cable loops through garment to secure it to fixture.

Figure 7–7 Mechanical-cable security fixture. (Courtesy of Protex International Corp., 390 Knickerbocker Avenue, Bohemia, NY 11716.)

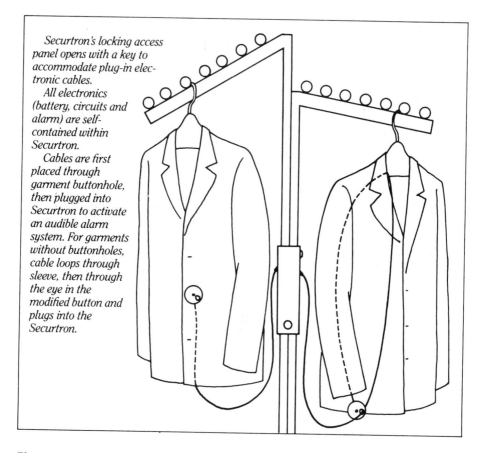

Securtron's locking access panel opens with a key to accommodate plug-in electronic cables.

All electronics (battery, circuits and alarm) are self-contained within Securtron.

Cables are first placed through garment buttonhole, then plugged into Securtron to activate an audible alarm system. For garments without buttonholes, cable loops through sleeve, then through the eye in the modified button and plugs into the Securtron.

Figure 7—8 Electronic-cable security fixture. (Courtesy of Protex International Corp., 390 Knickerbocker Avenue, Bohemia, NY 11716.)

which can be passed through garments and then secured to a locked receptacle affixed to the fixture. A simpler arrangement is to loop cable through the merchandise and around its fixture and then secure both cable ends with a small padlock. The electronic cable is somewhat more sophisticated. It consists of a number of small-gauge electric wires, which can be connected together and strung through garments, and whose ends terminate in an electrical alarm box that is controlled by a key (Figure 7–9). If one of the cables is separated from the others or cut, an alarm sounds. The control box key is required to silence the alarm. These cables are very effective at preventing shoplifting.

Fixtures

Numerous display fixtures are available today that are designed to protect the goods that they display. The most basic fixture of this type is a lockable showcase. Another

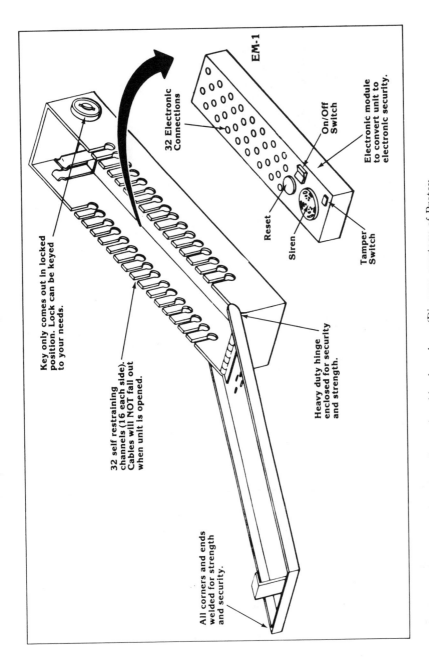

Key only comes out in locked position. Lock can be keyed to your needs.

32 self restraining channels (16 each side). Cables will NOT fall out when unit is opened.

All corners and ends welded for strength and security.

Heavy duty hinge enclosed for security and strength.

32 Electronic Connections

EM-1

On/Off Switch

Electronic module to convert unit to electronic security.

Reset

Siren

Tamper Switch

Figure 7–9(a) Diagram of an electronic cable alarm box. (Diagram courtesy of Protex International Corp., 390 Knickerbocker Avenue, Bohemia, NY 11716.)

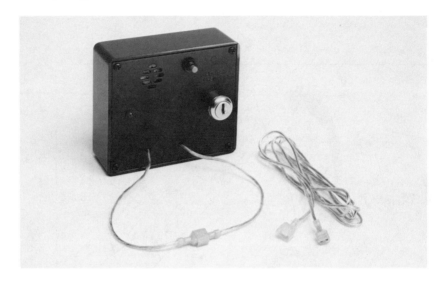

Figure 7–9(b) Alarm boxes for electronic cables. (Photo courtesy of Protex International Corp., 390 Knickerbocker Avenue, Bohemia, NY 11716.)

example of a security fixture is one designed to display and secure expensive belts (Figure 7–10). This fixture is both attractive and functional. Similar fixtures are designed to secure fashion jewelry, small leather goods, furs, women's handbags, and other like types of merchandise.

"Securatach"

These plastic ties can be purchased in any hardware or electrical supply store and used to secure an ordinary clothes hanger to a display fixture. The tie is passed through the small eye on the end of the hanger, and with the hanger on the rod or fixture, the tie is run past the rod and around the stem of the hook before the tie is cinched closed tightly (Figure 7–11). This is a simple and inexpensive means of securing the hanger to the fixture.

Closed-Circuit Television

The use of closed-circuit television (CCTV) for loss prevention and shoplifting control is not new. What is new, however, is the current generation of computer-controlled cameras and the sophistication of both the cameras and the associated recording equipment.

Closed-circuit television can be used in a very simple and inexpensive yet very effective way. The vulnerability of hidden corners and obstructed views of mer-

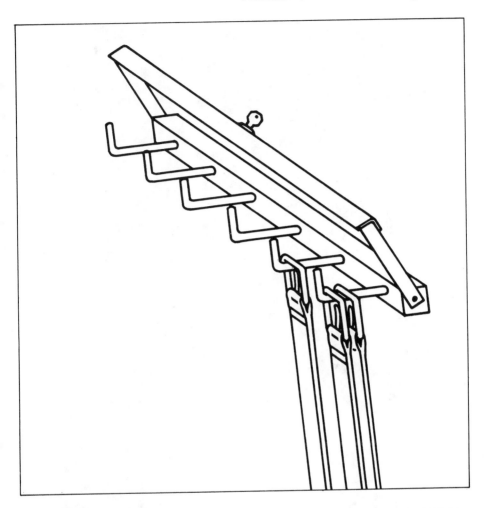

Figure 7–10 Securax belt fixture. (Courtesy of Protex International Corp., 390 Knickerbocker Avenue, Bohemia, NY 11716.)

chandise display areas to shoplifting have already been mentioned. Closed-circuit television can make these areas much less tempting to shoplifters while providing more complete sales floor coverage and better customer service. Simply install a CCTV camera to monitor the hidden area and connect it to a small (5″) television monitor in the cash register area. This arrangement provides the sales associates with a good view of the hidden area, thus making them aware of customers who need assistance and simultaneously alerting potential shoplifters that the area is under CCTV surveillance, deterring theft. This CCTV arrangement is not costly.

Figure 7–11   Securatach anti-shoplifting device.

Electronic Article Surveillance

Electronic article surveillance (EAS) is the formal name for the small plastic tags that merchants put on their merchandise.[1] The tag sounds an alarm when a customer tries to leave the store before it has been removed (Figure 7–12).

EQUIPMENT FOCUS

DATA SECURITY BANK

ELECTRONIC ARTICLE SURVEILLANCE SYSTEMS AND FLUID TAGS

Company	System	RF*	(Very low frequency) EM*	M*	(High frequency) MI*	HAM*	Fluid Tags	Features, Special Applications	Reader Service Number
CHECKPOINT SYSTEMS	Impulse program	•						Source tagging	141
	QS2000	•						Disposable tags, labels (for retail)	
	Alpha	•							
	Quicksilver	•							
	Signature Series	•						Wood sensors	
COLORTAG	ColorTag						•		142
	ColorTag Mini**						•	Delicate garments	
INTERNATIONAL LOSS PREVENTION SYSTEMS	Series 400	•						Single panel installation	143
KNOGO	Standard SRF System	•			•				144
	Ranger DRF Overhead	•						Covert, overhead	
	Chameleon Micro-Magnetic		•					Libraries, offices	
	Sentinel Micro-Magnetic	•	•						
	Silver Cloud SRF	•							
	Kno-Glo**						•		
MONARCH MARKING SYSTEMS	System One	•						Pricing and EAS system	145
	Mini-Loop System	•							
SECURITY TAG SYSTEMS	Sekurloop	•†						Anti-kidnapping, office equipment	146
	Sekurpost	•†							
	Sekurlabel	•†						Packaged goods	
	Inktag						•		
	Inktag II						•		
	Inktag III						•		
	Inkmate						•	Ink/EAS combination	
SENSORMATIC	AP600/Ultra-Max					•		Industrial (AP600)	147
	Aisle Keeper			•				Grocery stores	
	MicroMax				•				
	Standard Magnetic System			•					
	TellTag System	•						High-ticket soft goods	
	Sensorink**						•		
SENTRONIC INTERNATIONAL	Harmless to Health System			•				Floppy disks, tools	148
3M	Model 2600			•				Video stores	149
	Model 3300			•				Pricing and EAS system	

Key:

* RF = radio frequency, EM = electromagnetic, M = magnetic, MI = microwave, HAM = hybrid acoustic magneto

** = operates stand alone or interacts with sensors, † = uses very low radio frequency (frequency division technology)

Data are supplied in SECURITY Magazine's *Product, Service, Supplier's Guide* or from specification sheets. Information is as complete and correct as possible, yet non-response, market changes and other unintentional factors may affect content.

Source: SECURITY Magazine

Electronic article surveillance products allow retailers to maximize profits. Those seeking a wide detection range should consider radio frequency systems. Target choice contributes to the system's visibility and affects range.

Figure 7–12 Comparison chart for electronic article surveillance systems. (© 1991 *Security Magazine*. All rights reserved. Courtesy of *Security Magazine*.)

Until recently, EAS was the correct terminology for all these systems; however, the last few years have seen a new article surveillance technology develop that is not based on electronics but rather on a mechanical means of deterring theft. This new technology consists of a tag placed on merchandise that, if removed without the proper device, leaks an indelible ink that ruins the merchandise (Figure 7–13). The theory is that the presence of the tag, together with proper signage about the tag and how it works, deters people from shoplifting the item because of the certainty that it will be of no use if the tag is removed without the proper removal device. Merchants who use this device believe it works.

True electronic article surveillance, on the other hand, is truly electronic. The plastic tag placed on the merchandise also requires a special tool to remove it without damage to the merchandise. The tag contains a micro-electronic circuit or an electronic part that causes the tag to signal an alarm when it passes through a specific type of electronic or antenna field.

The newest innovation is what are commonly described as *smart tags;* if a shoplifter tries to defeat a smart tag while still in the store (in a fitting room, for example), it will, by means of self-contained electronics, emit a noise and an electronic signal that alerts store personnel that someone is attempting to remove the tag. Although expensive, these tags may be an appropriate way to prevent the theft of very expensive goods.

Although EAS systems have proved to be a very effective shoplifting deterrent, these systems are not without their problems. Perhaps the most troublesome one is the failure to remove (FTR) the tag on legitimate purchases. Nothing is as annoying to customers as discovering at home that an EAS tag was not removed in the store and can't be removed at home. Nothing hurts the store's image more. Another FTR problem—and one that has perhaps even more serious ramifications—is when the customer tries to leave the store with purchases, the alarm sounds, and an employee falsely accuses the customer of shoplifting. Such occurrences have produced successful lawsuits against retailers. The FTR problem is real; many experienced security practitioners will admit that for every EAS alarm for theft, there are 999 alarms for FTRs. This frequent exposure to civil liability and negative image is a factor that cannot be easily dismissed when contemplating the use of EAS. Store policy should be developed to determine in advance how such situations will be handled, and all personnel should be thoroughly trained in the procedures. In all cases, however, when an FTR causes an alarm, a store employee should apologize to the customer; delay and inconvenience should be minimized, and no words or actions should be used that give any hint that the customer was ever suspected of shoplifting. Some stores even hand the customer a preprinted apology and explanation of the incident (Figure 7–14).

Subliminal Messages

The use of subliminal messages broadcast over the store's public address or "music" system is highly controversial, and its effectiveness has not been proved. Its controversial aspects rise from its perception by many people as a mind-altering tech-

Figure 7–13 Dye released from Inktag anti-shoplifting device. (Courtesy of Security Tag Systems, Inc., PO Box 23000, St. Petersburg, FL 33742.

In an effort to control inventory losses,   utilizes an inventory control system. This system utilizes special inventory control tags which are attached to our merchandise and can only be removed by a special device.

Although we attempt to always remove these inventory control tags when a customer purchases merchandise, occasionally there is an oversight. When this happens, our system alerts a salesperson, which allows us to remove the tag and minimize any inconvenience or damage to your merchandise that would have resulted had you left the store with the tag attached to your purchase.

Thank you for allowing our Customer Service Representative to remove the inventory control tag. We apologize for any inconvenience. Using your receipt, we will identify the employee who handled your transaction and take the appropriate steps to insure that this does not recur, again please pardon the inconvenience.

Figure 7–14   Apology for failure to remove electronic article surveillance tags

nology that can be used for purposes other than to prevent shoplifting. For example, *if* subliminal messages are effective at deterring shoplifting, then why not use it to encourage shoppers to make more purchases? Because subliminal technology cannot be consciously perceived by those exposed to it, the potential for abuse is always present.

Aside from little data on its effectiveness, the most troubling aspect of subliminal technology for the retailer is perhaps the adverse publicity that might result should the public become aware of its use. Subliminal messages are mentioned here in the interest of thoroughness. It is an available technology, but we make no recommendation or claim for its effectiveness or appropriateness.

FITTING ROOMS

Fitting rooms are a particularly vulnerable area for theft because potential shoplifters have a feeling of anonymity and privacy in a fitting room, which heightens their sense of security and their belief in the store's inability to detect their shoplifting activities. Although the use of CCTV, two-way mirrors, peek-holes, etc., to observe the activity in a fitting room is legally prohibited in all jurisdictions that we're aware of and the violation of these prohibitions carries both civil and criminal liability, perfectly legal means can be used to minimize theft occurring in fitting rooms.

Standards and Procedures
Customer Service

Good customer service in fitting rooms is the best theft preventative. A customer who never knows when a salesperson will come in to the fitting room to offer assistance will be reluctant to stuff stolen merchandise in a shopping bag for fear of being caught. Of course, part of good customer service in fitting rooms is moving all merchandise left by customers back to the selling floor. Not only is this a theft prevention technique but also goods left in fitting rooms aren't available for sale to customers on the selling floor.

Clearing Fitting Rooms

A standard that requires that fitting rooms are cleared of merchandise frequently and regularly by sales personnel ensures that a customer entering the fitting room without any thought of committing a theft will not be tempted to steal garments left there by others. Goods left in fitting rooms are extremely vulnerable to theft, and therefore their frequent and systematic removal to the selling floor is essential.

Limiting Number of Garments

Another standard to consider is limiting the number of garments allowed in the fitting room at any one time. This limit enables employees to better observe what is being taken into the fitting room (they should assist the customer taking the goods into the fitting room) and to prevent a large accumulation of goods in the fitting room.

Fitting Room Checkers

A fitting room checker is a specific employee stationed inside the fitting room bank entrance whose responsibility it is to check each customer in and out of the fitting room and account for all garments taken in and out by each customer. Checkers often assign a specific fitting room to each customer, and they use various techniques for tracking the items brought in by each customer. Checkers often help keep fitting rooms clear of merchandise and assist in returning merchandise to the selling floor. In larger stores, checkers are frequently part of the security or loss prevention department.

Psychological Factors
Signs

The use of tastefully designed signs displayed in fitting room common areas or in individual fitting rooms can deter theft. For example, a sign that advises customers of the number of garments they may take into the fitting room is useful.

Another fitting room sign that helps deter theft states that fitting room areas are patrolled by uniformed and nonuniformed security personnel. The mere knowledge that the store may send security personnel through the area has a deterrent value. Some stores go so far as to post a sign in the fitting room area that states, "Shoplifting is a crime. We prosecute all shoplifters."

A final psychological ploy is to occasionally use the store's public address system to announce, "Security needed in fitting room 4." Of course, customers and potential shoplifters have no idea which fitting room is meant. If they don't observe a security presence, they assume that another fitting room was involved. Again, the possibility of discovery and apprehension deters theft.

Design and Layout

Fitting room design can deter or encourage fitting room theft. For example, fitting rooms that have floor-to-ceiling walls and floor-to-ceiling doors provide complete privacy and tend to contribute to fitting room theft. By designing fitting rooms with a space of 12″ to 18″ below the walls between the individual fitting rooms and the tops of the walls only about 5½′ to 6′ above the floor (Figure 7–15), you provide

Figure 7–15 Fitting room.

adequate fitting room privacy without providing a totally private and totally unobservable area from which to steal.

Many retailers find that installing so-called reverse-louver fitting room doors is also a theft deterrent (Figure 7–16). By installing doors with louvers that permit someone outside the fitting room to see into the fitting room, you remove the feeling of total privacy and the unhindered opportunity to shoplift. Of course, the use of

Figure 7–16 Reverse-louver fitting room doors.

either of these designs is appropriate only when fitting rooms are limited to customers of the same sex and where observation of the rooms is impossible from the selling floor or other public areas.

Another caution is to limit places for the shoplifter to hide price tickets and EAS tags that have been removed from merchandise. Caulking mirrors and molding is highly recommended; ash trays and waste baskets should not be provided in fitting rooms.

Because a sense of anonymity provides a sense of security that often tempts customers to shoplift, anything that can be done to remove this anonymity will help deter theft. A chime that sounds whenever someone enters or leaves the fitting room is helpful. Not only does the chime signal customers that their entrance into the fitting room has probably been observed but it also directs the salespeople's attention to the presence of customers in the fitting room, alerting them to the need for service. Likewise, when customers exit the fitting room, the chime alerts the sales associates to check for a sale or the need for assistance, and it makes the customers aware that sales personnel know they have left the fitting room.

Another technique that has been successfully used is to lock the entrance to the fitting rooms with an electrically operated strike plate. When customers require entrance to the fitting room, they are required to press a button next to the entrance door. This sounds an alarm by the cash register station, and the sales associate acknowledges the customer's presence and presses a button by the register. This electrically unlocks the fitting room entrance door (Dutch door or gate) permitting the customer access to the fitting rooms. What does this accomplish? It lets customers know that store personnel know they are in the fitting room, and it gives the sales associate a chance to see the customer and provide sales assistance.

A final important note about design: Banks of fitting rooms should have only one entrance that also serves as the exit. Do not allow customers to enter on one side and exit on the other.

Equipment

The use of numbered "discs" to control the flow of garments in and out of the fitting room is a recommended practice (Figure 7–17). Fitting room discs are used in the following manner: The fitting room checker carefully counts the number of garments a customer is taking into the fitting room. The checker then hands the customer a plastic disc (similar to the discs used to differentiate clothing sizes on a display rod) that is marked with the number of items the customer will try on. The customer presents the checker with the disc and the merchandise when leaving the fitting room. The checker compares the number of garments being removed from the fitting room with the number on the disc. If the checker's count matches the number on the disc, then the customer has brought out every item taken into the fitting room, ensuring that none has been stolen.

Figure 7–17 Numbered discs for use in fitting rooms.

Equipment is also available that electronically encodes each disc with the correct number of garments just before it is handed to the customer. This equipment precludes the customer from stealing a disc to use later for shoplifting.

When the disc system is used, the discs must be secured when not in use by locking them in an appropriate cabinet or drawer, and they must be carefully controlled during operating hours (Figure 7–18). Shoplifters have been known to keep or steal discs and to use them to defeat the control system.

STOCKROOMS

Stockrooms are not usually considered a place where shoplifting occurs because stockrooms are normally not accessible to the public. However, there is no better place for a shoplifter, especially a professional shoplifter, than a stockroom. The merchandise is neatly stacked, sized, and sorted. The stockroom is certainly private, unless an employee happens to come in. An experienced shoplifter can be in and out of a stockroom in less than 60 seconds with thousands of dollars in stolen merchandise. Fortunately, there are ways to prevent this potential loss.

Figure 7–18   Locking cabinet for numbered discs.

Standards and Procedures

The easiest stockroom standard to establish is to insist that employees challenge everyone in a stockroom who is not immediately recognized as an employee. Vendors, who are often properly permitted access to stockrooms, should be required to wear clearly identifiable visitor badges while working in stockrooms or other back areas of the store.

If a given stockroom contains both general merchandise and highly desirable, expensive, or high-shortage merchandise, such as expensive perfume in a cosmetic stockroom, it's a good idea to segregate the latter in a locked area. A large stockroom usually has heavy traffic; the objective should be to permit as little access as possible to very expensive merchandise. Segregating and locking up such items as furs and jewelry (which really deserve a vault for storage), leathers, video cameras, and small electronics in separate cages within a larger stockroom is a prudent procedure.

Psychological Factors
Signs

Signs outside and inside stockrooms may deter theft. Exterior signs should indicate that the area is for employees only and that access is restricted (Figure 7–19).

Figure 7–19 Restricted access sign for a stockroom.

These signs tend to discourage some potential thieves or customers from exploring the area out of curiosity, if for no other reason. They may also facilitate trespassing arrests, if necessary. Without such signage, the store may be unable to deal effectively with stockroom prowlers. Inside the stockroom, signs reminding employees to lock the door, to challenge strangers, and to keep accurate stock records all help to discourage theft.

Key Logs

A key log requires each person who opens a secured area (for example, a separate caged area within a stockroom that contains high-shortage merchandise) to sign a log indicating his or her name and the time and date. Some logs also require certification of the time the secured area was relocked. If losses do occur, the log is a handy tool for ascertaining who had access to the area. In any event, simply requiring the log reminds everyone entering the area of its security needs and reminds them that management is concerned enough to maintain such records.

Design and Layout
Locking

It is desirable to prevent unauthorized access to stockrooms. This can be accomplished by locking stockroom doors that open onto the selling floor. The best type of lock to use is a combination lock because it is easy to change the combination when employees leave or when the combination is compromised by carelessness

(Figure 7–20). A keyed lock requires the services of a locksmith whenever it must be rekeyed; combination locks can be easily changed by anyone.

Some stockrooms contain emergency exits leading to fire stairs, escape exits from the building, and so on. Such exits should be alarmed locally with a crash-bar buzzer alarm (Figure 7–21) or with an alarm that signals a continually staffed security office. The mere presence of these alarms will deter shoplifters from taking merchandise and exiting through an emergency door with it. This same principle applies to fire exit doors that lead from the selling floor.

Equipment

With high-value merchandise, it may be useful to cable or otherwise alarm it while it is stored in stockrooms. Another viable option is to use CCTV to monitor stockroom activity. Even the mere presence of cameras deters theft in stockrooms in the same fashion as on the selling floor; the ability to monitor stockroom activity also provides management with a valuable tool for monitoring productivity and other aspects of backroom operations.

SUMMARY

We firmly believe that efforts directed toward preventing and deterring shoplifting are of great importance. Many prevention efforts can often be accomplished with little or no attendant costs, and they often enhance or at least complement other desirable business goals. For example, what retailer isn't concerned with improving the level of customer service or having the merchandise displays appear neat and

Figure 7–20 Combination lock.

Figure 7–21 Emergency exit equipped with crash-bar buzzer alarm.

orderly? Perhaps an equally important reason for beginning anti-shoplifting strategies with prevention is that if the theft is prevented, there is no need to make detentions or apprehensions—activities that can be costly in terms of personnel and unanticipated legal fees. Modern loss prevention professionals are nearly unanimous in their belief that the key to minimizing shoplifting losses is not detecting and apprehending multitudes of shoplifters but establishing an effective prevention program that deters most thefts, thereby requiring that only the determined or hardcore shoplifter need be dealt with by apprehension and prosecution.

NOTE

1. Some of the leading companies that have been in the business of manufacturing and installing EAS systems include the following.
   a. Sensormatic Electronics Corp., Deerfield Beach, Fla.
   b. Knogo North America, Hauppauge, NY.
   c. The 3M Company, Minneapolis, Minn.

8

Mechanics of Detection and Apprehension

Regardless of the policies and procedures established by management for apprehending shoplifters, specific prerequisites should be met before an apprehension is made, and other crucial actions should be integral to the apprehension. When adroitly executed, this blend of prerequisite conditions and subsequent actions results in a legal apprehension with minimal risk of either injury to the parties involved or subsequent civil action.

SIX STEPS TO APPREHENSION

As indicated in Chapter 6, six requirements must be met to justify an apprehension for shoplifting. (*Shoplifting* is used here in its classical sense, that is, carrying goods out of a store. There are interesting variations of shoplifting, and the mechanics of their detection and apprehension will be addressed later in this chapter.)

1. See the suspect approach the merchandise.
2. See the suspect take possession of the merchandise.
3. See where the suspect conceals the merchandise.
4. Maintain an uninterrupted surveillance to ensure that the suspect doesn't dispose of the merchandise.
5. See the suspect fail to pay for the merchandise.
6. Approach the suspect outside the store.

These six steps do not necessarily reflect any statutory requirements. However, if each of these steps are followed, it's hard to imagine how a false arrest or mistake could occur.

Before we analyze each of these steps it's important to note and comment on this issue of maintaining an "uninterrupted surveillance." There are a growing number of cameras that are monitored in a room away from the selling floor, and to a lesser extent, surveillance windows or booths, that require the security operative to disengage from the surveillance and travel to the location where the suspect is in the store. Obviously, in these situations, the surveillance is interrupted. The rule of constant and uninterrupted surveillance applies to situations where an article has been *concealed*. If a suspect has selected an item and the security agent disengages from the remote surveillance location and arrives on the scene prior to concealment, the interruption may not be a factor. Further, if radio contact allows a second security agent to maintain the surveillance after concealment, "patching together" a continuous surveillance, if you will, the rule of uninterrupted surveillance has not been broken and the subsequent detention is valid. The second agent is obviously a part of and witness to the event.

Step 1: See the Suspect Approach the Merchandise

It would be ideal if the suspect could be observed entering the store. Then the frequent claim of having brought the merchandise into the store to refund or exchange it would be ineffective. The next best condition would be to see the customer enter the department or area of the store from which the actual theft occurred. More often than not, however, these conditions cannot be met. At a minimum, the customer must be seen approaching the location where the merchandise is normally displayed.

Too often, employees have come upon the scene to observe a customer with merchandise already in hand. They assumed that the merchandise was being shoplifted. As events unfolded, it turned out that the customer had brought the goods back to the store to compare, for any number of reasons, or was engaged in making an unauthorized but not illegal exchange. For this reason, employees must comply with the rule of observing the customer approach the merchandise.

Step 2: See the Suspect Take the Merchandise

Perhaps the most important element of this step is the first word. The employee who attempts to apprehend the suspect must *personally* observe the suspect take at least one item of merchandise. An apprehension should never be based on the observations or the word of another person, whether a fellow employee or a customer. It is absolutely mandatory that the theft be observed by the person apprehending the suspect.

Legally, the term *taking* has a specific meaning. For this discussion, it simply means physically taking merchandise into one's possession and moving it with the intent to steal it. The intent to steal can be demonstrated by such things as concealing the goods or removing price tickets or electronic article surveillance devices. Of course, it goes without saying that the merchandise taken must belong to the store. The theft of property that does not belong to the store (for example, the theft of a customer's wallet by a pickpocket), although constituting the crime of theft, is not shoplifting. The special rules established to protect merchants from civil suits resulting from confronting suspected shoplifters often do not apply to such thefts.

It is important to be certain that the property in question belongs to the store for another reason. Con artists occasionally attempt a scam in which they make the shoplifting of merchandise obvious. When they are subsequently apprehended, it turns out that the "merchandise" was planted in the store earlier, and the con artists can prove it is their property. Although in most jurisdictions criminal or civil statutes provide some protection to security agents who make an apprehension under such conditions, these con artists hope for a quick cash settlement, relying on the merchant's fear of adverse publicity and the time and costs involved in establishing the facts through the courts.

For these reasons, plus the fact that nearly all jurisdictions require personal observation of misdemeanor crimes (including shoplifting) before an arrest can be made, the personal observation of the theft by the security agent or sales associate making the apprehension is mandatory. Although it is true that some laws allow merchants to detain and question shoplifters without their personal observation of the theft, we prefer to follow the old security professional's adage: "If you didn't see it, it didn't happen." Following this advice is the safest course of action, and we recommend no other.

Step 3: See Where the Suspect Conceals the Merchandise

Shoplifters normally conceal shoplifted items in some manner. They may put the item in a bag, hide it under their clothing or in a pocket, and so on. In some jurisdictions (Nevada, for example), the concealment of an item taken is prima facie (on its face) evidence of the intent to shoplift. Occasionally, however, shoplifters do not conceal the stolen goods. Some shoplifters simply wear or carry the stolen property out of the store. Stolen necklaces, earrings, and rings are sometimes worn out of the store. This method is also occasionally used to shoplift outerwear. Although stolen goods are usually concealed, the failure to conceal stolen merchandise does not render the theft less criminal or less able to be prosecuted. It makes sense that the observing employee must know where the merchandise has been concealed. If the goods have "disappeared" or the employee is unsure of their location, then perhaps the goods disappeared somewhere other than on the customer's person or in his or her possessions. This requirement only strengthens the case.

Step 4: Maintain an Uninterrupted Surveillance to Ensure That the Suspect Doesn't Dispose of the Merchandise

Constant surveillance from the time of the theft to the time of apprehension is essential for four reasons:

1. To preclude the suspected shoplifter from disposing of the merchandise because of a change of heart or out of fear of detection. If this happens, the shoplifter will not have any stolen goods in possession when stopped, and thus the door is opened to a civil suit for false arrest.

2. To ascertain if the stolen merchandise is passed off to an accomplice. The accomplice may be equally guilty of shoplifting, depending on whether he or she took an active role in the theft or knew that the merchandise was in fact stolen before taking possession of it.

3. To observe any additional thefts by the shoplifter.

4. To be certain that the suspect does not eventually pay for the "stolen" item before leaving the store.

Step 5: See the Suspect Fail to Pay for the Merchandise

As obvious as it may seem, this step is sometimes overlooked by people who consider themselves proficient in retail security. In a recent case, two grocery store detectives observed a man hide a package of meat down the front of his jeans. The detectives left the store and waited for him to exit! How many times has a thief been foiled or scared by someone they mistakenly suspected of being security or the police or management? How many times has a person intended to steal and at the last moment, abandoned their plan, and paid for the merchandise for some reason?

Step 6: Approach the Suspect Outside the Store

It is recommended that the shoplifter be allowed to leave the store before being apprehended. This is generally not a legal requirement, but it is a practical one. Because the crime of theft is a specific intent crime (one that requires the mental formation of the intent to do the act, as opposed to doing something negligently or inadvertently), it is helpful in establishing intent when the shoplifter leaves the premises with the stolen property. This action disproves any subsequent claim that the shoplifter intended to pay for the merchandise. If apprehended in the store, shoplifters can claim that they were looking for another item to match the shoplifted one or that they were looking for a friend to obtain a second opinion before purchasing the item. These claims might be believed unless the shoplifter has left the store without paying for the goods.

In some circumstances it may not be practical or desirable to wait to make the apprehension until the shoplifter leaves the store. In some cases, such as ticket switching or fraudulent refunding, it may be appropriate to apprehend the suspect before he or she leaves the store. There is normally no legal obstacle to doing so, provided that the security agent can articulate the factors preceding the apprehension that clearly demonstrate that a theft occurred and that the suspect had formulated the requisite intent to commit the theft.

CONFRONTATION

Once the decision has been made to approach and confront a suspected shoplifter, we enter the next important phase following detection: apprehension. Although the word *confrontation* accurately describes the act of coming face to face with the shoplifter, it is not meant to carry the connotation of defiance and hostility sometimes associated with the word. The act of coming face to face with a shoplifter might just as properly be called the *approach*, except that the word lacks the implication of continuing action after the initial approach and identification procedures. The initial contact with the shoplifter should not be overly aggressive in tone or manner, it should not be combative in nature, and it should not be overtly confrontational. Initially, the confrontation should be done calmly and professionally, with an air of authority that subtlely lets the shoplifter know that the employee is in psychological and physical control of the situation.

The confrontation is discussed in its logical components: the approach, the identification, the request, and the establishment of control.

The Approach

Whenever possible, the store representatives present during the approach should outnumber the shoplifter suspects by at least one. For example, if there are two shoplifter suspects, it would be desirable for three store representatives to make the approach. This advantage in numbers immediately helps establish a psychological and physical control of the situation. The presence of the additional employee helps deter the suspect from using force to resist the apprehension, and the additional person can serve as a witness to corroborate testimony about the manner in which the suspect was apprehended. If a female suspect is to be apprehended, it is preferable to have at least one female store representative present as a witness.

Whenever more than one employee is involved in the approach, one person should be in charge and speak with the suspect while the others act as a back-up and as witnesses. Several people all talking at once is both confusing and unprofessional. The person in charge faces the suspect while the second person assumes a position to the right and slightly to the rear of the suspect. This places the assistant out of the direct view of the suspect, and it should help deter an escape attempt. Should the suspect attempt to fight, the assistant can easily grab and immobilize the suspect from the rear (holding force).

The store representatives who approach a suspected shoplifter should be alert for associates or accomplices who may be waiting for the shoplifter and who could pose a danger to the apprehending agents. The agent in charge should approach the shoplifter head-on to block the escape route and to force him or her to stop.

The Identification

Immediately after the approach, the apprehending agents must identify themselves. Especially today, with the frequency of daylight muggings and assaults committed in public view, any fear that the shoplifter is about to be mugged or assaulted by two people who suddenly approach and block the way must immediately be put to rest. The person in charge should immediately identify him- or herself as a representative or security agent of the store. For example, the agent might say, "Excuse me, sir. I'm with ABC Stores, and I would like to talk to you about the blue shirt in your bag." Such identification notifies the shoplifter about who you are and what the confrontation is about. At this point, shoplifters often make some spontaneous remark such as, "Oh, I'm sorry. I forgot to pay for it." It's important to make a mental note of these comments and quote them in the subsequent report. Don't accuse the suspect of theft, and don't use such words as *steal* or *shoplifter*. They are inflammatory and serve no useful purpose. If necessary, reference should be made to a "problem" that needs resolution.

If security personnel make the apprehension, they should display a badge when identifying themselves. This symbol of authority is universally recognized, it visually establishes the identity of the apprehending agents, and it helps establish psychological control of the situation.

The way the store representatives conduct themselves while making the apprehension has a significant influence on how the shoplifter behaves. The identification process is perhaps the most critical in the apprehension process, and whether the procedure will be a smooth one or a rocky one is often determined at this point.

The Request

The identification should be immediately followed by a statement such as, "Would you mind coming back into the store with us so we can clear this matter up?" Even though the shoplifter is asked to accompany the agents back into the store, the request should be made in a tone of voice that indicates it is really a demand. Putting the demand in the form of a request is less antagonistic, and if a mistake has been made, it may tend to mitigate some tort actions. The apprehending employees should gently guide the shoplifter back into the store and to a place where the offense can be discussed in private. Avoid grabbing the suspect or trying to pull or push the suspect into the store; such actions could constitute either excessive force or battery, and it looks bad to other customers or members of the public who observe the incident.

The discussion with the shoplifter is normally held in the security office or the manager's office. In any event, it should be held in a private place beyond the view of the public.

The Establishment of Control

Superiority in numbers and an authoritative manner will give the store representatives the physical and psychological control of the shoplifter in most cases. How should the other cases be handled?

Some juveniles and some adult shoplifters, usually professionals or repeat offenders, will not succumb to the request to return to the store because they do not want to be arrested. They may already be on probation for a prior offense, and another conviction will mean a jail sentence, or they may be wanted for other crimes and fear discovery if arrested for shoplifting. Some juveniles feel that shoplifting is a game and if they can outrun the apprehending person and escape detention, they will have a great story to tell their friends. For these and a variety of other reasons, a few shoplifters will attempt to escape by simply running away or by fighting. Unless the apprehending people are well trained security agents, the best course of action is usually to swallow your pride and let the suspect escape.

In many of these situations, the shoplifter abandons the stolen goods, so the store gets its merchandise back, perhaps none the worse for wear. Even if the merchandise is not recovered, it is important to keep a sense of perspective. Is it worth getting injured for a $3.27 steak or even a $500 coat? Chances are good that shoplifters who escape will not revisit the store; they have been identified and will prefer to ply their trade in the future where they are not known. Although no one likes to be bested in whatever we do, sometimes discretion is truly the better part of valor. Well-trained security personnel are better equipped to deal with such shoplifters. Most security agents carry and are trained in the use of handcuffs, and they will use these tools of the trade in appropriate situations.

TICKET SWITCHING AND FRAUDULENT REFUNDS

Ticket switching and fraudulent refunding are "nonclassical" shoplifting techniques. Ticket switching is simply replacing a price ticket from a lower priced item for the ticket of a higher priced item in the hope that the salesperson will not notice the incorrect price. Fraudulent refunding is shoplifting an item and immediately taking it to a sales person for a cash refund, usually by claiming that the reason for the lack of a sales receipt is that the item was received as a gift.

Steps to follow on a ticket switch:

1. Observe the suspect approach and select both items.
2. Observe the suspect remove or obliterate the price of the more expensive item.
3. Observe the suspect remove the price tag or ticket from the lower priced item.
4. Observe the suspect affix the lower price ticket onto the more valuable item.
5. If possible, recover the higher price ticket and the lower priced merchandise as evidence.
6. Observe the customer present the merchandise for payment.
7. If the cashier or salesperson questions or challenges the price, do not interfere. Do not instruct the cashier to sell the item at the lower price. If the sale is denied in the normal course of events, take no action.
8. If the item is purchased at the lowered price, detain the suspect.
9. Retain the following for evidence: two price tickets, two items of merchandise, and one receipt.

Steps to follow on a fraud refund:

1. Observe the suspect approach the merchandise.
2. Observe the suspect taking the merchandise.
3. Know where the merchandise is.
4. Maintain uninterrupted surveillance until the suspect presents the article for a refund.
5. If it is a charge transaction—that is, if credit is issued to an account—stop the suspect after the transaction has been completed and before he or she departs from the transaction area.
6. Evidence for a charge transaction consists of the following: the article of merchandise that was presented for refund, the container, if any, used to transport the stolen item (other than a personal handbag), and the credit document.
7. If it is a cash refund transaction, stop the suspect as he or she picks up the cash.
8. Evidence for a cash transaction consists of the following: the article refunded, the container in which the stolen article was carried, the cash that was being disbursed, and the cash refund document.

The approach, the identification, the request, and the establishment of control are the same for these thefts as in the more common shoplifting act.

SUMMARY

When choosing the appropriate course of action when shoplifting is suspected, several criteria must be met before detaining or apprehending a suspect:

- The suspect must be observed approaching the merchandise, and any packages or other items in his or her possession should be noted mentally.

- The suspect should be kept under constant observation from the time of the theft until the apprehension.
- What the suspect does with the stolen merchandise is very important. Is it concealed or worn out of the store? The agent should be able to describe to the shoplifter exactly what was taken and where it is at the time of the apprehension.
- The shoplifter should normally be permitted to leave the store before being detained.

The confrontation with the shoplifter is perhaps the most critical portion of the detection and apprehension process. In the initial confrontation, the store representatives should be polite but firm. It is desirable that the representatives outnumber the shoplifters by at least one. If a female shoplifter is to be apprehended, a female employee should be present as a witness. Store representatives should clearly identify themselves to the shoplifter and state in simple terms why they are there. They should ask the suspect to accompany them into the store to "clear the matter up." Avoid harsh accusations whenever possible; guide rather than grab or shove the suspect into the store. A firm, polite, and businesslike manner that exudes confidence will convince most suspects to follow directions peacefully.

At the moment of confrontation, store representatives must establish physical and psychological control over the suspect. This is best accomplished by superiority of numbers, a confident no-nonsense attitude, and positioning that discourages fighting or fleeing.

Remember, the entire process of detection and apprehension is designed to get the shoplifter to return willingly to the store where the stolen property can be recovered and a decision made regarding the disposition of the suspect.

SUGGESTIONS FOR FURTHER READING

Dozens of source materials deal with the detection, apprehension, and disposition of shoplifters. Listed below are only a few of the materials that may be of interest and may provide different perspectives and emphasis.

Chamber of Commerce. *Probable Cause*. Los Angeles: Anti-Shoplifting Education Campaign Subcommittee, Los Angeles Area Chamber of Commerce, 1977.
French, J.T. *Apprehending and Prosecuting Shoplifters and Dishonest Employees*. New York: National Retail Merchants Association, 1979.
Kaufmann, Arthur C. *Combatting Shoplifting*. New York: National Retail Federation, 1974.
Sklar, Stanley L. *Shoplifting—What You Need to Know about the Law*. New York: Fairchild Publications, 1982.

9

Processing the Shoplifter

Once the shoplifter has been detained, the subsequent procedures, which comprise the processing of the case, are as important as the steps that must be followed prior to the detention. A perfectly proper detection and apprehension can be fatally tainted in terms of prosecution and can invite subsequent litigation if the processing isn't handled correctly. Pages of examples could be offered on how improper processing has come back to haunt retailers. One example should suffice to make the point. In one case, a shoplifter was prosecuted for stealing a bottle of whiskey. The evidence, the whiskey bottle, wasn't properly tagged or marked. At the trial, as a result of this processing mistake, the bottle could not be produced or positively identified as the one the defendant allegedly took. Without the evidence, the matter was dismissed, the shoplifter walked away, and the store was exposed to civil litigation.

Processing the shoplifter includes the following steps:

- escorting the offender to the office
- processing the offender in a private location
- witnessing the processing
- restraining the offender in the office
- handling personal requests
- documenting the incident
- obtaining a statement
- preserving the evidence
- processing the evidence
- photographing the shoplifter and the evidence
- deciding whether to accept restitution
- deciding whether to allow a conditional release

ESCORTING THE OFFENDER TO THE OFFICE

The ultimate objective is to move the offender as quickly and quietly as possible to the security of the room where the processing will take place. Two employees should escort the shoplifter to the office. They should walk slightly behind but close to the offender, representing a physical and psychological barrier to discourage the offender from turning and fleeing. Everything within reason should be done to return to the store with as little fanfare as possible. As they progress through the store, the security agents might conduct a soothing conversation aimed at disarming and calming the suspect, whose mind is probably racing with alarm.

If the shoplifter tries to bolt while inside the store, the risk of injury is great. Glass display cases, fixtures, and merchandise may be broken. Broken glass on hard and potentially slippery floors can be extremely dangerous. Not only is the welfare of employees a concern but also that of the shoplifter and, even more important, the innocent customers. Pursuing a shoplifter in the parking lot and its attendant risks have already been discussed. A pursuit inside the store holds even greater risks, and management must consider them when developing individual policies.

PROCESSING THE OFFENDER IN A PRIVATE LOCATION

Shoplifters should be processed in an office or other designated area where the privacy of the proceedings can be ensured. The processing should be conducted out of the sight and hearing of the public and of the employees who are not involved in the matter. Most retailers don't have the luxury of an office dedicated to security use, hence some other office should be designated for this purpose and vacated on demand.

WITNESSING THE PROCESSING

From the time the shoplifter is returned to the store until that person is escorted out by the police or otherwise leaves the store, two employees should be present. One of the employees who made the detention is usually the witness to the theft. The second employee need not have any information or knowledge of the theft itself; he or she is simply present to observe the proceedings passively and to be available, if required, to provide a statement about the shoplifter's treatment during the detainment in the store. If the shoplifter is female, one of the employees should also be female. This strategy is aimed at countering false claims of sexual harassment. All documentation generated during the processing should bear the date and time and the names and signatures of the witnesses.

The Question of Courtesy

Retail security practitioners know there are times when it takes great inner strength to overcome the temptation to return verbal abuse, be sarcastic, or use profanity when dealing with some shoplifters. It is the mark of a professional to overcome such temptations. Both of the authors have dealt with this issue in different ways. This is our advice: kill them with kindness. If they're obnoxious, you need not stoop that low. Kill them with courtesy. If they are upset, embarrassed, or ashamed, your courteousness will help reduce their pain. Be kind. They lost, and you won. Be professional. Treat every shoplifter just the way you would like to be treated.

RESTRAINING THE OFFENDER IN THE OFFICE

Only use handcuffs to restrain a shoplifter in the office if it's necessary, that is, if the failure to use them would likely result in violence. Some stores have security offices equipped with bars or rings specifically designed to accommodate handcuffed suspects. Many stores opt to handcuff suspects to a chair. Whatever the method, it shouldn't be followed or used routinely. Not all shoplifters require handcuffs. Discretion should be used.

HANDLING PERSONAL REQUESTS

Personal requests such as asking to use the rest room, requesting a drink of water, use of the telephone, and so on must be dealt with courteously but firmly. Normally, such requests should be granted if reasonable and if they do not pose a safety or escape risk. The use of a telephone should be postponed until processing has been completed. Smoking by a detained shoplifter during processing should not be permitted.

DOCUMENTING THE INCIDENT

The first post-apprehension consideration is adequately documenting the entire incident, from the events leading up to the apprehension to the details of the apprehension itself. This documentation will provide the cornerstone of any subsequent prosecution, and it will lay the foundation for a defense should a civil suit result from the apprehension.

To successfully prosecute a shoplifting offense, the prosecuting authority (the district attorney or the state's attorney) must be able to establish all the elements of the crime. The merchant's documentation of the observations and the facts leading up to the apprehension is the vehicle that the prosecutor uses for this purpose. It is therefore essential that the documentation be clear and detailed, free of conjecture and speculation, unbiased, and totally factual.

A good written report of an apprehension contains just the facts. After the apprehension, the individuals who stopped the suspect must write down the observations that led to the arrest of the shoplifter. This report should also detail any other evidence supporting the arrest, such as price tickets surreptitiously removed and discarded by the shoplifter, or the employee's observation of the shoplifter entering the store with an empty bag, which was subsequently used to secrete the stolen merchandise. Figure 9–1 shows a sample apprehension form.

Any statements made by the shoplifter that are inculpatory should be quoted verbatim. When first approached by a store representative, shoplifters often realize that their theft has been detected, and they instinctively make a statement such as, "I was going to pay for it" or "I'll give it back." Such statements are incriminatory, and they must be quoted accurately and be properly reported in the documentation of the apprehension. For example, a report might state: "When initially approached outside the front door, the suspect immediately said, 'OK, I'll give you your stuff back.' " Should the shoplifter later deny his guilt, this spontaneous statement will refute his claim of innocence.

Documentation is also useful in defending against civil actions; many of the prosecutorial requirements are equally applicable in defending civil suits. It is not unusual for a perfectly valid shoplifting apprehension to be declined for prosecution by the local prosecutor. If the case load of serious crimes is particularly heavy, a nonviolent misdemeanor may be pushed aside for the sake of expediency. As a result, the shoplifter may sue the merchant on the belief that the failure to prosecute is proof of a false arrest. Legally, such is not the case, but a well-documented report covering the initial apprehension may be sufficient to convince the shoplifter or the shoplifter's attorney that the arrest was valid, thus forestalling litigation before it gets off the ground.

The documentation of apprehensions, including any photographs or evidence obtained in connection with the apprehension, should be retained in a secure manner for a period of at least five years. The actual merchandise being held as evidence may normally be returned to stock after 2 years, provided such merchandise is photographed and those photos are retained with the file.

OBTAINING A STATEMENT

In addition to noting the shoplifter's pertinent comments about the theft in the documentation of the incident, it is desirable to obtain a signed statement from the shoplifter admitting the crime. This confession must be entirely voluntary to meet various legal requirements. It cannot be obtained as a result of threats, coercion, or promises of rewards. For example, any statement obtained in return for a promise not to call the police would be illegally obtained and not worth the paper it was written on. An easy way to obtain a signed statement is to have a preprinted form available, such as the ones shown in Figure 9–2.

STORE	SECURITY APPREHENSION REPORT		TYPE OF CASE			
			SL	FA	MA	CA

ADDRESS	CASE NO. —CHAR. of CASE	AGENT NAME AND ID NO.

PHONE	CHARGE	ARREST DAY/DATE	TIME OF ARREST

SUSPECT LAST NAME	FIRST NAME	MIDDLE INITIAL	PUBLIC ☐ EMPLOYEE ☐

HOME ADDRESS	CITY	STATE	HOME PHONE ( )

DATE OF BIRTH	AGE	SOCIAL SECURITY NO.	DRIVER'S LICENSE NO.	SEX	MAIDEN NAME/ALIAS

Prosecuted ☐ Released ☐	PREVIOUS MACY ARREST—CASE NO./DATE	OTHER ARRESTS	NAMES Cross-Filed

RACE	HEIGHT	WEIGHT	COLOR HAIR	COLOR EYES	MARITAL STATUS	OCCUPATION	EMPLOYER

MARKS OR SCARS	WEARING AND WHAT CARRYING (Full Description, Colors, Etc.)	PD CASE NO.	TIME PD CALLED
		DATE OF APPEAR-ANCE	TIME PD RESPONDED

HANDCUFFING INFORMATION ☐ On Contact ☐ In Office ☐ No	ADMISSION CARD SENT? ☐YES ☐NO	AWARD ☐YES $ ____ ☐NO LOG NO.	EVIDENCE ☐ Booked ☐ Held	DIV CK ☐ YES ☐ NO	SPA CARD SENT ☐ YES ☐ NO	CD LETTER SENT ☐ YES ☐ NO	PHOTO TAKEN ☐ YES ☐ NO

Dept. No.	Class No.	Style No.	Quantity	Description of Merchandise	Location Codes	Unit Price	Total Value
						TOTAL $	

FACTS (INCLUDE ALL ELEMENTS OF CRIME, BY WHOM OBSERVED, AND TIME OF OBSERVATION.) USE REVERSE SIDE FOR CONTINUATION

Note: Explanation of selected sections above:

Type of Case: Shoplifting, Fraud, Miscellaneous, Check (Arrest)
Case No.—Char. of Case: For businesses using a case numbering system.
Admission Card Sent: Did suspect sign admission of theft card?
Award: Was award paid to any employee? Amount.
Div. Ck.: Were company records checked for prior offense?
SPA Card Sent: Was record sent to any Store Protective Ass'n or other private record-keeping entity?
CD Letter Sent: Was Civil Demand letter sent?

SIGNATURE OF ARRESTING AGENT	SIGNATURE OF AGENT MAKING REPORT	SECURITY AGENTS ASSISTING INITIALS
	APPROVED BY:	FOR OFFICE USE ONLY ENTERED BY: ____ DATE ____

Figure 9–1 Security apprehension report.

VOLUNTARY STATEMENT

Date_____

    I, _____, freely admit that on the above date I took the following items from (name of store) without paying for them with the intent to convert them to my own use.

    (Description of item[s])   (Retail price)

_____

_____

_____

_____

Total number of item(s) taken_____

Total value of item(s) taken_____

    I am signing this admission of theft freely and voluntarily and without any threats, coercion, or promise of reward having been made as an inducement to obtain my signature.

_____
(Signature)

Address: _____

               _____

Phone:_____

_____
(Witnessed by)

_____
(Time)

Figure 9–2 Voluntary statements.

SECURITY REPORT

STATEMENT

Date_____

I, the undersigned do voluntarily admit and state that on this date I entered the store, located at the address indicated below, where without making payment therefor, I took and carried from the possession of said store, without consent, the following property:

STORE	STORE NUMBER	STREET		CITY		STATE

Item	Price

TOTAL_____

I, the undersigned, in signing this statement and surrendering the aforementioned items, do so voluntarily and of my own free will and without force or threats or promises of any kind and with the understanding that I fully release the above-mentioned store or company and all its agencies and representatives individually and personally from all types of civil liability.

MAKE THIS REPORT IN DUPLICATE
SEND ORIGINAL TO

Signed_____
FIRST   MIDDLE   LAST

RETAIN DUPLICATE FOR YOUR FILE

Address_____

WITNESSES

_____   _____
NAME   NAME

PLEASE PRINT   PLEASE PRINT

LAST NAME		FIRST	MIDDLE
MAIDEN NAME AND OTHER NAMES USED:			
STREET ADDRESS		CITY	STATE
TELEPHONE NUMBER	OCCUPATION	EMPLOYED BY:	
SOCIAL SECURITY NUMBER	DRIVER'S LICENSE	IMMIGRATION NUMBER	

SEX	RACE	DATE OF BIRTH: MONTH DAY YEAR	AGE	1 – UNDER 12 2 – 12-17
1____ MALE	1____ CAUCASIAN 2____NEGRO	HEIGHT WEIGHT HAIR EYES		3 – 18-29 4 – 30-39
2____ FEMALE	3____ ORIENTAL 4____ OTHER			5 – 40-49 6 – 50-59
				7 – OVER 60

DESCRIBE METHOD OF OPERATION: _____

1 – PURSE	2 – SHOPPING BAG	3 – OTHER BAG	For Regional Use Only
4 – PROFESSIONAL	5 – POCKET	6 – PRICE SWITCHER	
7 – ACCOMPLICE	8 – UNDER CLOTHING	9 – OTHER	

STATEMENT OF SUBJECT: _____

WAS SUBJECT RELEASED?	WAS SUBJECT BOOKED?	WHERE WAS SUBJECT BOOKED?		WAS THE EVIDENCE BOOKED?
DATE	CIRCLE ONE	MONDAY 1 TUESDAY 2 WEDNESDAY 3 THURSDAY 4	FRIDAY 5 SATURDAY 6 SUNDAY 7	
TIME OF DAY	1 BEFORE NOON 4 6:00 P.M. TO 9:00 P.M.	2 NOON TO 3:00 P.M. 5 9:00 P.M. TO MIDNIGHT	3 3:00 P.M. TO 6:00 P.M. 6 AFTER MIDNIGHT	

1 – FRESH MEAT	2 – DELI	3 – OTHER FOOD ITEM	TOTAL NUMBER OF ARTICLES
4 – LIQUOR	5 – CIGARETTES	6 – VITAMINS	
7 – DRUG	8 – CLOTHING	9 – OTHER NON-FOOD ITEM	TOTAL VALUE OF ARTICLES

TO BE SIGNED BY PERSON WHO MADE THE APPREHENSION

_____   _____   _____
SIGNATURE OF APPREHENDING PERSON   TITLE OR POSITION   TELEPHONE

Obtaining a signed statement is normally not difficult. Suspects should simply be advised that they have been apprehended for shoplifting and that as a routine part of the processing and to keep the record accurate, you would like them to sign a statement listing the items that they took so that there will be no confusion at a later date. In most jurisdictions, a statement obtained by nonpolice personnel need not contain an admonition or a warning. Check with your attorney or local prosecutor before finalizing the format of any such statements. In any event, the confession should be filled out, and if the shoplifter refuses to sign it, a notation to this effect should be written in the signature block. The form should be retained and filed with the other case documentation.

PRESERVING THE EVIDENCE

A successful criminal prosecution and a successful civil litigation defense require evidence that supports the contentions of the offering party. A well-prepared, detailed report of the shoplifting incident is essential, but a report that is backed up by the very items recovered from the shoplifter lends credence to the retailer's claims.

The prosecuting authority requires such physical evidence, whether it be the actual items recovered or photographs of them. Suffice it to say that any merchandise recovered from the shoplifter and any other items that tend to prove the offense must be retained in their original condition in a manner that prevents tampering or alteration until they are required at the trial. What items other than recovered merchandise might prove useful? Any other object that played a part in or tends to prove the offense should be preserved, for example, the empty shopping bag carried into the store by the suspect or the price tickets removed and discarded by the shoplifter. If the shoplifter used any device or tool to aid in the theft, such as wire cutters used to remove a security device, these items must also be preserved as evidence. All physical evidence should be thoroughly described and listed on the apprehension report.

As already mentioned, all evidence should be stored in a manner that prevents tampering or alteration. A special locked cabinet or storage area should be used solely for the purpose of holding evidence, and access to this area should be strictly controlled. Ideally, each piece of evidence is placed in a sealed container on which it is noted when the container is opened, by whom, and why, and the disposition of the evidence after handling. Obviously, the preservation of perishable evidence such as meat or dairy products requires special attention.

PROCESSING THE EVIDENCE

The primary purpose of any evidence procedure is to ensure that the "chain of custody" is maintained. The proper maintenance of this system protects the evidence from being successfully challenged when introduced in a court of law.

Some jurisdictions allow photographs in lieu of physical evidence. This is of major economic importance to retailers because it does not require that merchandise involved in an apprehension be pulled off the selling floor and stored for long periods of time. Therefore, retailers are strongly encouraged to contact the local district attorney's office to determine if photographs are admissible and to obtain any specific requirements (for example, the size of photographs). A duplicate set of photographs must be taken and kept in the possession of the security department.

The evidence procedure described here is based on the use of a log book and property tags. All evidence must be stored in a secured location in the store.

The Log Book

The log book is divided into 12 columns, which are set up as follows:

1. The first column is for the case file number.
2. The second column is used for the name of the suspect, date of birth, date of arrest, charge, and arresting agent.
3. The third column indicates the merchandise department number.
4. The fourth column is for the merchandise description.
5. The fifth column is used for the merchandise color.
6. The sixth column indicates the merchandise size.
7. The seventh column includes the merchandise price.
8. The eighth column indicates the date the merchandise was put into evidence storage.
9. The ninth column indicates the date the evidence was removed to be brought to court.
10. The tenth column indicates the date the evidence was returned from the court.
11. The eleventh column indicates the date the merchandise was taken out of evidence storage.
12. The twelfth column indicates the reason why the evidence was removed from storage.

All evidence must be logged in black ink. "DATE OUT" and "REASON OUT" for all entries must be logged in a different color ink.

Evidence will be logged out for the following reasons:

1. "To court for trial"
2. "The case has been adjudicated." The results of prosecution—for example, one year county jail and five years probation, case dismissed, etc.—will also be logged in the "REASON OUT" column.

Refund merchandise will have one of the following "REASON OUT":

1. Merchandise returned to customer.
2. Recovery per Security; merchandise returned to stock.
3. Bank check sent to customer. Merchandise returned to stock.

When identical items of merchandise are entered in the log, each separate item must be listed. If the items are absolutely identical (the same color, size, etc.), the information may be printed once and ditto marks placed on the lines beneath. However, only one item of merchandise may be listed on each line. To ensure clarity and neatness, skip two lines between each case.

Figure 9–3 shows a sample page from an evidence log book.

Property Tags

After the evidence is boxed or bagged and sealed, a property tag must be attached to the box or bag. The tag must be filled out as follows:

1. SUSPECT: Print or type the name(s) of the suspect(s).
2. CHARGE: Penal code section of the crime committed.
3. DATE: Date of apprehension.
4. ARRESTING OFFICER: Name of agent who made the arrest.
5. CASE FILE NUMBER: This number is the permanent case file reference number.
6. DESCRIPTION OF PROPERTY: This need only be a general description because there is a complete and itemized list of all property in the evidence log book.
7. CUSTODY LOG

    DATE: This is the date the evidence is moved to or from the evidence storage area.

    IN/OUT: State whether the evidence is being removed or returned to the evidence storage area.

    TO: State where the evidence is being taken, that is, court, stock, etc.

    BY: Signature of the individual transporting the evidence.

When evidence is removed from the store, the property tag should accompany the evidence. All movement must be indicated. Use the reverse side of the tag if necessary. The property tag should be destroyed when the merchandise is returned to stock. Remember that the property tag preserves the "chain of custody." Figure 9–4 shows sample property tags.

PHOTOGRAPHING THE SHOPLIFTER AND THE EVIDENCE

The practice of photographing suspects after apprehension is recommended so that their identity is firmly established. It is not uncommon for shoplifters to use false identification; a photograph of the person apprehended removes any subsequent doubt in terms of identity. A photograph from an "instant" camera is recommended. It can be initialed, dated, and referenced to the appropriate apprehension report,

PAGE # _____

EVIDENCE LOG

CASE #	SUSPECT'S NAME, DOB, DOA, CHARGE, ARRESTING AGENT	DEPARTMENT NAME OR #	MERCHANDISE DESCRIPTION	COLOR	SIZE	PRICE	DATE IN	DATE OUT TO COURT	DATE IN FROM COURT	DATE OUT	REASON OUT
SL91-008	SMITH, James, 9-19-61, 1-2-91, 484 P.C., Lombard	46	Umbrella	Black	N/A	39.99	1-2-91	1-10-91	1-12-91	1-15-91	Guilty plea 1 year probation

Figure 9–3 Evidence log.

PROPERTY TAG

Suspect_____

Charge_____Date_____

Arresting Officer_____

Property No.

Description of Property

_____

_____

_____

Custody Log

Date	In/Out	To	By

F59-04 2/72

PROPERTY TAG

Suspect SMITH, JAMES A.

Charge 484 PC Date 1-2-91   SL 91-008

Arresting Officer ADAMS, GEORGE

Property No.

Description of Property

ONE BLACK UMBRELLA - FOLDING TYPE

Custody Log

Date	In/Out	To	By
1-10-91	OUT	COURT	G. Adams
1-12-91	IN	EVIDENCE	G. Adams
1-15-91	OUT	STOCK	G. Adams

Figure 9–4 Property tags.

thus eliminating any delay in obtaining the actual photograph and reducing the possibility of subsequent confusion or misidentification. The suspect's name, the date, the time, the dollar value of the stolen goods, and the names of the people making the apprehension should be written on an 8″ × 11″ piece of paper with a felt-tip pen and taped to the wall behind the shoplifter when the photo is taken. This data should be clearly visible in the picture. It is not uncommon for a shoplifter who has been caught to subsequently purchase duplicates of the stolen items; when the court date arrives, the shoplifter can produce a receipt for the goods that were stolen and claim that a mistake had been made. The data shown in the photograph can negate such a claim since today many cash register receipts show the date and time of purchase.

When allowed by the prosecutor, the advantages of photographing evidence are clear. First, the merchandise can be returned to stock for sale, and its value isn't lost while it sits in an evidence locker. Second, maintaining the care of the chain of evidence isn't a factor. Finally, much storage space isn't required.

DECIDING WHETHER TO ACCEPT RESTITUTION

In most cases, *restitution* means that the shoplifter simply pays for the items he or she attempted to steal. The question of whether to accept restitution from a shoplifter has advocates on both sides of the issue. We believe that accepting restitution is not a good idea for a few reasons.

First, many prosecuting authorities are reluctant to prosecute if restitution has been made. Although a theft was attempted and thwarted by the merchant, in the eyes of many prosecutors, the incident was settled as a civil matter by the merchant's acceptance of restitution. Many criminal juries feel similarly; thus, restitution risks a successful conclusion to a criminal case.

Second, the merchant's handling of the shoplifting incident is more open to question if money changes hands between the shoplifter and the apprehending merchant.

Another, but equally important concern, is the temptation for some security or store personnel to accept "restitution" money from the shoplifter in exchange for not prosecuting and allowing the suspect to go. Many shoplifters will ask to be permitted to pay for the stolen items and to be given another chance. In our opinion, any policy that permits the acceptance of restitution at the time of arrest in such an emotionally charged atmosphere encourages problems. The potential for trouble is reduced by prohibiting any sort of restitution payment.

Fourth, the merchant usually recovers the stolen goods, which negates the need for any restitution unless the merchandise has been damaged. Under these circumstances, the acceptance of any payment, other than for the purchase of the stolen items, constitutes a fine or penalty that the merchant cannot legally assess or receive. If a restitution payment were made and the payment influenced the merchant's decision not to prosecute, most jurisdictions would consider such an arrangement extortion. Extortion is a criminal offense for which the merchant could be charged.

Finally, if restitution is in order, most prosecutors will ask the court to order restitution as part of the sentence meted out to the offender.

DECIDING WHETHER TO ALLOW A CONDITIONAL RELEASE

Many merchants are caught in a dilemma when they consider the alternatives available to them after apprehending a suspect for shoplifting. The decision of whether to prosecute or release a shoplifter can be difficult. Many merchants would like to find a middle ground; they are not particularly enamored of the idea of prosecution and the concomitant time required for court appearances, but neither can they simply forgive and forget. The conditional release may be an answer to this dilemma.

In essence, the conditional release is a formal way for the merchant to tell the shoplifter: "You're getting a break this time. We're not going to call the police and have you prosecuted. However, we do not take this incident lightly. You have committed a crime and stolen from us. We have the next 12 months in which to seek prosecution for the crime you have committed. We are putting you on notice to this effect. Provided you do not steal from us again, after 12 months this incident will be closed. However, if you are caught stealing from us again within 12 months, we will not only prosecute you for that theft but for this incident as well."

To formalize this arrangement and to make an adequate impression on the shoplifter, a conditional, or release form is recommended (Figure 9–5). The form is signed by the suspect, and he or she is given a copy. In many cases, the conditional release serves the merchant's interests and the shoplifter's. Most shoplifters are amateurs; once caught and properly admonished, they do not repeat the offense.

LENGTH OF THE PROCESSING PROCEDURE

How long should processing a shoplifter take? Are there reasons for limiting the time? Is there harm in using the processing procedure to inconvenience shoplifters and thus "teach them a lesson"? In fact, there are limits on how long the processing should take, and the procedure cannot be used punitively.

Most state laws require that the processing of a shoplifter be done within a reasonable amount of time and that once this amount of time has expired, the shoplifter must be either released or turned over to the police. There are no definitive guidelines defining "a reasonable amount of time." However, after 60 minutes the limit is being tested. Each situation is unique, and the reasonableness of the time used will be judged on the totality of the circumstances pertaining to each particular incident. The best procedure is to handle the processing as expeditiously as possible but not with such haste that essential procedures are neglected or carelessly executed. The processing of a shoplifter must be handled in a thoroughly businesslike fashion; scoldings, lectures, recriminations, and threats should be avoided.

A note of caution: In the event of a "bad stop" or "questionable detention"— that is, an innocent person has been detained for shoplifting or the shoplifter has

Date _____

You, _____ , have been detained by
Security Employees for shoplifting. This act is a violation of the California Penal Code,
Section 484, relating to theft.

Our action in releasing you at this time does not constitute a waiver of our rights to file
a criminal complaint and pursue prosecution. Our review of the facts surrounding this case
will be completed by _____ .
If we decide to initiate prosecution, you will be notified on or before the above date by
the police or the court. At that time, you will also be told where to appear to surrender
for fingerprinting and formal booking procedures.

The crime of theft has a statute of limitations of one year. Your release today or a decision
not to pursue criminal prosecution during our review does not waive our right to institute
criminal prosecution for this incident should another act of theft be committed by you at
any   store during this one year period.

In addition, your release without criminal prosecution does not release you or your legal
parent/guardian from any civil redress available to   under applicable state laws.

Do not call the store to discuss the details or inquire about the status of this matter. Store
policy prohibits anyone from discussing the matter with you while the case is under review.

_____   Date _____
Signature
Releasee ☐   Legal Parent/Guardian ☐

_____   Date _____
Witness

DISTRIBUTION: WHITE COPY – File   YELLOW COPY – Releasee

Figure 9–5 Controlled release form.

been clever enough to dispose of the stolen goods without being seen—it is vital that the person be released with the least amount of delay possible. After obtaining the individual's name (which may be needed in the future should any repercussions arise from this incident) and making the appropriate apologies, the store representatives should allow the person to go. If they wish to stay and discuss the matter, they should politely but firmly be led from the store and taken outside to a public sidewalk. If they persist, the representatives should attempt to politely extricate themselves from the discussion. If this is impractical, the discussion should take place as unobtrusively as possible in a public area where it is clear that the person is not being detained and is free to go. Although holding such a discussion in a public place is not desirable, it is preferable to doing so inside the store, where individuals could claim to have been detained against their will or that they were required to engage in the discussion.

It is not uncommon for people who have been detained for shoplifting to claim that they were held for an excessive period of time. We've seen wild exaggerations in this regard. Hence, it's only prudent to record the time at which

- the shoplifter was first observed
- the theft occurred
- the shoplifter left the store
- the shoplifter was apprehended
- the shoplifter arrived in the office
- the police were called
- the police arrived
- the shoplifter left the store

If these times are duly noted as a matter of policy and are witnessed by two employees, the shoplifter's claim of being detained for an excessive period of time can be successfully refuted.

SUMMARY

When shoplifters are processed, they are in every sense of the word deprived of their liberty and under the control of store employees. What happens, how it happens, how long it takes, what is said by all parties, and virtually everything that transpires during processing is important. Issues such as the use of force or any touching of the detainee, privacy, courtesy, witnesses, documenting times, preserving the evidence, photographing the shoplifter, discussions or arrangements for restitution, admissions of guilt, and the eventual release of the suspect must be made a matter of permanent record. The times of each facet of activity should be documented, from the initial confrontation outside the store to when the police removed the subject from the office. If all activities and the times of each are duly noted, the matter will be viewed as having been professionally managed.

10

Supervising Security Personnel

Supervision is synonymous with *direction, surveillance,* and *guidance.* When supervising security personnel, all of the items in this triad must be used for effective management.

DIRECTION

Those who manage security operations must begin supervising security personnel by giving clear direction to their activities. Good direction starts with a thorough review of the company's policies and procedures and thorough training in the techniques of shoplifting, the mechanics of detection and apprehension, and the proper processing procedures. In other words, supervisors must provide the security agents or employees responsible for security activities with solid training. The training must be accompanied by a means of ensuring that the training material has been understood and absorbed by the trainee; any form of review and testing accomplishes this requirement. When the training phase is properly completed, the direction element of the supervision triad has been fulfilled.

SURVEILLANCE

The surveillance portion of the supervision triad is the real guts of supervision. One cannot supervise without frequently and closely observing the employees being supervised. How else is the supervisor to know what's happening? Simply reviewing reports or records (as obligatory and essential as this is) never provides adequate knowledge of employees' activities. Only frequent and detailed personal observation of all of the activities of security personnel will provide a level of supervision that satisfies legal and business requirements.

How does a supervisor achieve an adequate level of observation? Good supervision doesn't have to be oppressive or overbearing, but it does have to be frequent, detailed, and performed by a knowledgeable person. Thus, the supervisor must be fully knowledgeable in all aspects of the activities under observation. Unless skilled observers are used, deviations from accepted practice or specific company-directed security policies and procedures may not be detected.

An objective of supervision that goes beyond simply ensuring compliance with the procedural aspects of the job is that of ensuring that the more abstract and philosophical desires of management are being met. These desires are best established by a written statement setting forth management's expectations and standards. For security personnel, such a statement of expectations could be found in the following set of standards:

STANDARDS OF CONDUCT FOR SECURITY PERSONNEL

The standard of conduct expected of security personnel should be such that no person will have cause to question your character, honesty, integrity, or discretion. In the performance of your duties, you must be highly professional and must meet more exacting standards of behavior and adherence to rules than others. The nature of your function, authority, and responsibility requires this higher standard.

The following types of behavior are not in keeping with our Standards of Conduct for security personnel:

1. Any misuse of company equipment or property, misuse of position or authority, or agreement to accept "favors" not granted others and available or offered to you because of your position is prohibited. Covered under this statement are such things as the following:
    a. Use of company phones for personal calls.
    b. Removal of company property for personal use.
    c. Use of parking validation cards, stamps, machines, etc., to avoid personal nonbusiness parking charges.
    d. "Borrowing" company property for any purpose without proper documentation and approval.
    e. Taking advantage of your position to secure favored treatment with regard to obtaining merchandise or any other advantage not granted to other employees.
    f. Any misuse of company security ID or badge.
2. Failure to objectively and factually report information required or obtained within the scope of employment. This statement covers not only the willful misstatement of facts but also knowingly omitting pertinent information from reports or purposefully "slanting" or "coloring" reports.
3. The failure to report any information, however obtained, that could conceivably bear on or be pertinent to any security investigation or be of legitimate interest to company management.

4. Failure to submit reports as required by company policy.
5. Violation of any of the provisions of the company "Use of Force or Weapons" policy.
6. Any misuse or careless or improper handling of funds, evidence, company property, or records entrusted to your care.
7. Any activity that reflects adversely on the ethical or professional stature of you or the company. Covered under this statement are such activities as:
    a. Improper or inappropriate language in dealing with suspects or employees.
    b. Any activity that could be construed as entrapment.
    c. Any activity that is designed to harass or embarrass an individual and that has no other legitimate purpose.
    d. Discussion or disclosure, by any means, of past, pending, or proposed security investigations or activities with people who do not have a legitimate need to know.
    e. Misuse or unauthorized disclosure of company confidential information, such as personnel or security information, obtained in the course of your employment.
    f. Mistreatment or abuse of people in custody.
8. Failure to follow company policies and procedures with respect to stopping, questioning, or apprehending employees or the public.
9. The failure to be completely truthful and candid in response to any official request for information.

The above statements are not intended to cover all situations, rules, policies, procedures, regulations, etc., and should not be construed as such. They are, however, indicative of the spirit and intent of the company's policy and the expectations of your conduct and behavior. These standards are of such importance that any person failing to comply with them will be subject to disciplinary action, including discharge without warning.

Maintaining the standards outlined above and the philosophical framework created by them should be the guideline in your professional approach to your daily activities.

I HAVE READ AND UNDERSTAND the Standards of Conduct outlined above. I understand these standards are not intended to establish any express or contractual rights. I also understand that any violation of these standards may result in disciplinary action, up to and including termination of my employment without prior warning.

_____

Name (Print)

_____   _____

Signature   Date

These Standards of Conduct can be modified to reflect individual company standards and should be reviewed by the human resources or personnel department and perhaps by legal counsel. The form that follows the Standards should be signed by all security employees, and a signed copy should be placed in their personnel files.

Written standards of conduct provide employees with guidelines on the behavior expected of them and to which they will be held accountable. It also provides the employer with a written acknowledgment that employees were advised of and fully understand the standards of the employer.

GUIDANCE

The last element of the triad of supervision is guidance. Whenever a supervisor discovers that an activity is not being performed properly or up to expectations (assuming that the errant behavior does not warrant discipline or termination), the supervisor must counsel and provide remedial guidance to the subordinate. In this stage of the supervisory process, good employees can be made into outstanding employees. Here the old adage "As the twig is bent, so the tree grows" comes into play. Good supervisors offer friendly advice, suggestions for improvement, and nurturing; they are generally supportive and helpful, but they also demand and obtain corrective action when required. Anyone with knowledge can criticize and find fault with someone who is less experienced; it is *how* supervisors deal with such situations that determines not only their worth as supervisors but also the future value and productivity of their employees.

Most authorities[1] agree that successful supervisors have four basic qualities:

1. Technical mastery. This simply means acquiring greater understanding and more facts about all aspects of the job than those who will be supervised.
2. Skill in planning. Supervisors must think ahead about both technical and non-technical matters and use the product of this planning to assist in efficiently accomplishing the task at hand.
3. Skill in human relations. This skill covers all aspects of a supervisor's job because the results the supervisor obtains depend largely on how other people perform. The ability to motivate others is a major part of the supervisor's role.
4. Skill in interpreting and administering policies. Obviously, a supervisor who is not fully versed in the details of the company's policies and who does not have a full understanding of the philosophy behind them cannot adequately supervise others.

SUMMARY

Too little has been written about supervisory training for security professionals. Suffice it to say that every effort should be made to formally train security supervisors to properly prepare them for their important responsibility of getting the job done through line employees. Without training, how can a newly appointed supervisor understand how to conduct a store detective's performance appraisal or how to handle a disciplinary interview in a positive and constructive way? These situations are the windows through which the supervisor can be evaluated.

The supervisor's steadying hand and attention to the employee's needs should be evident in the employee's work. Every report prepared by the security officer should be marked with the supervisor's signature or initials and the date of the review. Every personnel and security training file should contain notes reflecting the oversight and involvement of the supervisor. The supervisor's signatures and notes document the existence of meaningful supervision.

The supervision of security personnel requires the following:

1. A knowledgeable and skilled supervisor.
2. Initial direction and training to provide the foundation on which the supervisor will build and develop the employees.
3. Frequent and thorough observation and auditing of the employees to ascertain that they understand and are following the policies and procedures established by the employer during the initial training. Observation must be done with the goal of detecting deficiencies, but criticisms should always be helpful and constructive. Supervision should be close but not overbearing.
4. Guidance for employees to assist them in achieving excellence and exceeding company expectations of performance and conduct.

NOTE

1. Paul Pigors and Charles A. Myers, *Personnel Administration—A Point of View and a Method,* 3d ed. (New York: McGraw-Hill, 1956).

11

Handling Questionable Detentions

"To err is human; to forgive divine."[1] Unfortunately, only the first half of Pope's equation is always true when a suspected shoplifter is detained in error. Errors are occasionally made despite rigorous training and supervision. When innocent customers are detained as suspected shoplifters, some may not initially be disposed to forgiveness. They want retribution, and a civil lawsuit is one popular way to obtain it. Obviously, lawsuits are time consuming, expensive to defend, and distracting for the merchant, and they should be avoided when possible. The merchant's task therefore is to do everything possible to prevent the customer from believing that a lawsuit is the only option available for redress of an injury or affront.

The detention of a person wrongly identified as a shoplifter is commonly known as a *false arrest;* some people argue that depending on local laws it may fall short of an arrest and be only a "detention," but these distinctions are, as a practical matter, artificial. When someone is erroneously stopped for shoplifting, for all intents and purposes they have been falsely arrested. This may be an actual crime, but more often than not, it is viewed as a tort (a civil wrong) for which the offended party may seek legal redress in the form of financial damages.

Errors made in detaining an innocent person for shoplifting are often referred to as *bad stops,* a phrase we do not encourage or endorse. This term indicates that something "bad" has happened, when more realistically, something "questionable" has happened. Invariably, the customer has been a player in the incident, albeit innocently. The industry has struggled for years to find a suitable label for this unfortunate occurrence. Other common terms include *possible false arrest, customer*

137

contact, and *nonproductive detention (NPD).* We recommend that such incidents be referred to as *questionable detentions* because this is the most accurate term.

The necessity of documenting all aspects of detentions and apprehensions was discussed in Chapter 9. That need is as applicable to questionable detentions as it is to justified detentions. When a questionable stop has occurred, the merchant, however innocent and well intentioned, has made a mistake. Exacting documentation made at the time of the event is essential because the mistake will have to be examined and explained. Detailed documentation is also important in assisting management to assess the seriousness of the incident and to determine the best course of action to resolve the matter.

TYPES OF QUESTIONABLE DETENTIONS

There are two categories of questionable detentions: The first category contains the customer who is truly an innocent party but whose conduct, for any number of reasons, led the security employee to believe that a theft had occurred. People in this category are innocent victims of circumstance.

Here is a classic example of how a false arrest can occur: A customer purchases a scarf on Monday, and on Tuesday she decides the color is not to her liking. She puts the scarf in her purse to return it to the store. In the store, she approaches the counter on which scarves are displayed. She removes her scarf from her purse to compare it to the merchandise. She's observed by a security agent at this point. The customer decides the color is fine after all, and she returns the scarf to her purse. She is stopped as she exits the store.

There are virtually limitless variations that could occur inside a store and lead to a questionable detention, hence the importance of following the six steps to apprehension.

The second category contains the customer who is not truly an innocent party but for any number of reasons is not in possession of the stolen merchandise when stopped by the security employee. Like it or not, this customer is entitled to be treated the same as customers in the first category. Category 2 customers tend to be more indignant, more offended, and more outraged than category 1 people.

The possible scenarios that could lead to this type of questionable detention are endless, but two examples should make the point. A customer intentionally secretes a small bottle of perfume in her coat pocket. As she turns the corner around the fragrance counter, she makes eye contact with another customer whom she suddenly suspects is a store detective. She's convinced she's been seen stealing. Indeed she has, but not by the customer she suspects. She decides to dispose of the perfume. She approaches another display and deftly slips the bottle under other goods. The security agent's view is momentarily blocked by other customers, and he doesn't see this. The customer is stopped outside the store, but she has no perfume.

Another customer purchases a pair of sunglasses and carries them with the receipt from the store. In his automobile, he removes the glasses from the small bag and re-enters the store with the bag in his jacket pocket. The receipt is still inside the bag. He approaches the display, removes an identical pair of sunglasses, and slips them into his jacket pocket and into the empty bag. He's stopped upon leaving the store. When asked to surrender the sunglasses he was seen taking, he removes the bag with the glasses and the receipt and claims to have purchased them.

Experienced retail security agents often know or sense the difference between category 1 and category 2 customers. Herein lies a problem. They know the former are innocent and just want to get away from the scene, but they have a different response to category 2 people. They often become angry because it's a professional slap in the face to be outsmarted by a thief. Their anger and resentment make it difficult for them to treat the two types of detainees the same, yet they must.

HANDLING A QUESTIONABLE DETENTION

What should be done to minimize the damage caused by a questionable detention? Four independent actions can ameliorate the situation:

1. Avoid an accusatory confrontation.
2. Avoid the use of force.
3. Courteously admit the mistake.
4. Disengage quickly.

Avoid an Accusatory Confrontation

If the recommended procedures for apprehending a suspected shoplifter are followed, some damage is automatically minimized. Apprehending personnel should always be mindful that mistakes are possible. Therefore, they should approach suspected shoplifters with an attitude that is as nonaccusatory as possible until they ascertain that the suspects have the stolen merchandise in their possession. The initial nonaccusatory approach is best made by following the apprehension techniques outlined in Chapter 8.

Avoid the Use of Force

The second action that will minimize damage from a questionable detention is to abstain from using force. Some situations may require limited force, but most people stopped for shoplifting are not violent and acquiesce to the directions given by security agents. The absence of force removes one more element of potential damage claims when a mistake is made.

Courteously Admit the Mistake

The next factor, which is very important in minimizing damages resulting from questionable detentions and should be present in all contacts with customers, is politeness. Politeness assuages many wrongs, and it is vital in minimizing the hurt suffered by falsely accused people. A sincere apology for the error is mandatory. To make an error and dismiss it without an apology simply adds insult to injury. The apology should be sincere and immediate and offered by the person who made the error. Subsequent apologies by store executives or owners may be appropriate follow-up, but the initial apology is vital. Many potential lawsuits from questionable detentions have disappeared when sincere apologies were immediately offered by the offending employee and followed up by a letter of apology and perhaps a dozen red roses or a store gift certificate.

Disengage Quickly

The final action for minimizing the damage from questionable detentions is to disengage from the contact once it has been determined that an error has been made. Immediately upon discovering that the suspect has not stolen anything, the store employee who made the detention should apologize and leave the scene. The customer who wants to discuss the matter further should be directed to the store manager's office. The customer should never be taken to or accompanied to the store manager's office; such actions could later be construed (or distorted) as maintaining custody or control of the customer.

If the customer is in the security office when innocence is established, he or she should be politely asked to leave. At this juncture, security agents and store employees are often tempted to explain or justify their actions to the customer. This temptation must be resisted. The customer and the employee are both in a state of heightened emotion; this is not the time to attempt to resolve the mistake. Customers who want to use the phone should be directed to a public phone in a public area of the store. Store employees may offer the necessary change to make the call, but they should essentially leave the customer alone in the area. Do not let the customer remain in the security office to use the phone or for any other reason. If the customer's identification has not been obtained, it should not be requested. If the customer pursues a complaint or legal action, his or her name will be clear from the documentation of the incident.

CUSTOMER INTERACTION AFTER THE EVENT

What should be done if a wrongly detained customer calls or writes the store to complain? First, a relatively senior executive or official should deal with the communication, but at least initially, there should always be a higher level executive to whom the complaint may be referred should the initial response prove inadequate. In other words, always leave an avenue for appeal and review of any initial decisions or discussion.

At every level, admit the error. Nothing is gained and much can be lost by taking the position that the problem was caused by the customer. A frank admission of error accompanied by a sincere apology and an offer to make amends often resolves the matter. Some customers are satisfied by an apology from an appropriately high-level manager. Other customers may ask for a written apology. Some may specify a particular sum of money. When this happens, management must decide how far to go to resolve the matter. Here is where a fully documented report of the questionable detention is extremely important. It will help management assess the nature and extent of the contact, identify any contributing factors resulting from the customer's actions, and provide some sense of just how badly the customer was damaged.

Questionable detentions can progress as follows:

1. no subsequent complaint
2. telephone call from customer or relative
3. letter from customer
4. telephone call from customer's attorney
5. letter from customer's attorney
6. summons and complaint indicating the filing of a lawsuit

The customer may demand money to satisfy the complaint through a call or letter or through the attorney. In any event, it is desirable to resolve the matter at the earliest stage possible. It is generally easier to deal with the customer than with the attorney. When an attorney gets involved, costs rise because now both the customer and the attorney must be compensated. Once a lawsuit has been filed, costs escalate rapidly, so all reasonable efforts should be made to avoid this eventuality.

Should the store involve its attorney or insurance carrier in these early negotiations? This question must be answered by the store's management in cooperation with the lawyer and insurance company. However, our experience has shown that until an impasse is reached or a lawsuit is filed, it is better to deal with the customer directly. When the store involves its attorney or insurance carrier, many customers feel the need to do the same in self-defense. The object in these cases is to resolve the matter as quickly and as amicably as possible; after all, the store is dealing with a customer, and the customer's goodwill and continued patronage are important.

A word of caution on the subject of letters of apology: It is important that such letters be sincere, but it is also important that they do not provide ammunition for the customer in the event that settlement arrangements break down and a lawsuit is filed. Letters of apology should therefore be relatively general and should not make what would amount to legal admissions of false arrest, negligence, use of excessive force, defamation, or other criminal or tortious conduct. An appropriate letter might be similar to the following:

Dear [name of customer]:

I want to apologize both personally and on behalf of [name of store] for the incident that occurred on [date] between yourself and our employees. We sincerely regret any embarrassment or inconvenience you suffered as a result of that incident. Rest assured that the employees involved have been appropriately counseled.

We want you to know that we value your patronage, and we trust that our error will not adversely impact the trust and confidence you have shown us in the past. We sincerely hope that our pleasant relationship will continue.

Please accept the enclosed gift certificate as a tangible token of our sincere apologies and regret concerning this incident.

The letter should be signed by a vice president or store manager.

The important thing to keep in mind about questionable detentions is that a mistake was made; a person was wrongly accused (either directly or by implication) of a crime. An occurrence such as this is an inconvenience and embarrassment and, even if handled politely and properly, can be traumatic. Assuming that the error was made in good faith, that is, the security agent or store employee had a reasonable basis for making the detention, the responsibility for the error rests on the store, and the customer cannot be blamed for it. Using reports of the incident, the store management must thus assess the seriousness of any damages to the customer apart from the original mistake itself and then determine how best to resolve the issue.

Every business that engages in apprehending shoplifters will at some time detain someone in error. If the business has well-planned and well-defined shoplifting apprehension policies and procedures, if the employees charged with apprehending suspects are well trained, and if the questionable detention is handled properly, actual damage to the customer is minimized. However, the customer can complain that they were stopped without legal justification, and various factors can give credence to such claims. Therefore, in the interests of controlling legal exposure and expense and maintaining the goodwill of the customer, it is important to deal honestly and forthrightly with such situations. Apologies and, if appropriate, some tangible form of compensation for the inconvenience and embarrassment resulting from such situations are in order. Nine times out of ten, the sincere, intelligent, and thoughtful handling of questionable detentions will avoid legal action, undue expense, and perhaps most important of all, the loss of a valued customer's goodwill.

LAWSUITS FOR QUESTIONABLE DETENTIONS

Knowing how to deal properly with questionable detentions will prevent an initial mistake from being compounded into a very costly series of mistakes that can only be resolved in a court of law. As we said, nine times out of ten, a lawsuit can be avoided. What about that tenth time?

When served with a summons and complaint or other legal document that certifies that you have been sued, you must contact your insurance carrier and legal counsel immediately. Most jurisdictions provide a relatively short time in which the defendant must respond or lose the suit by default. Hence, contacting your attorney quickly is essential. Most retailers carry liability insurance policies that cover the types of torts resulting from erroneous shoplifting detentions. Your insurance carrier will be a close partner in the defense of such lawsuits and may directly participate by providing counsel or indirectly by suggesting counsel.

Lawsuits take years to reach the courts, so it is imperative that all documents, memoranda, reports, etc., be preserved. The individuals involved should also be available for consultation with legal counsel. If an involved employee leaves your employ, their whereabouts should be kept up to date so that they can be located for testifying should the case come to trial.

In our experience, most lawsuits are never tried; they are settled out of court before the trial. Whether a case is settled depends on an agreement being reached between the opposing parties. The insurance carrier often makes specific recommendations in this regard.

Lawsuits over questionable detentions are always filed against the business. The security agent or employee directly involved may be named as a defendant, but the suit is primarily directed against the business for two reasons. First, the business is held responsible (absent certain very specific sets of circumstances) for the actions of its employees when they act for and on the behalf of the business. Second, the business has the money from which an award for damages can be obtained. Most security employees do not have the financial resources to support a substantial financial judgment, but an established and profitable business does.

SUMMARY

From time to time, people are stopped by security agents or retail employees in error. These questionable detentions typically fall into one of two categories: (1) the customer is truly an innocent party, or (2) the customer is not truly an innocent party. Irrespective of the category, the detaining party should avoid accusing the customer of wrongdoing, should avoid the use of force, should courteously admit the mistake, and should disengage from the situation quickly. There's nothing to gain, at any level, by denying that an error was made. Be circumspect in the choice of words if a letter of apology is sent. Sooner or later, stores that engage in shoplifting detection activity will make a questionable detention. Nine out of 10 times, a lawsuit can be avoided if it is properly handled.

NOTE

1. Alexander Pope, *An Essay in Criticism*, vol. II (London: W. Lewis, 1711).

12

Civil Recovery

Civil recovery is a generic term describing laws currently on the books in 36 states that were patterned after the original "civil demand" statute passed by Nevada in 1973. The Nevada law and those modeled on it allow retailers (and in some states other types of businesses and institutions, such as libraries) to demand money from people they have apprehended for shoplifting. The intent of these laws is twofold: to help compensate the merchant for the heavy costs of security and anti-shoplifting efforts and to act as a deterrent to shoplifting.

The passage of civil recovery laws is usually accompanied by heavy doses of media attention designed not only to advise citizens of the new law but also to remove some of the temptation to shoplift, thereby acting as a deterrent. Shoplifters who know that if they are caught, whether they are prosecuted or not, they can be required to pay up to $500 in penalties frequently have second thoughts about shoplifting.

State laws vary, but in most jurisdictions, the demand for civil remedy by a merchant is independent of whether the shoplifter has been criminally prosecuted. The merchant may demand restitution in either case.

THE CIVIL RECOVERY PROCESS

When a shoplifter is apprehended and caught with the goods, the merchant must decide whether to call the police and initiate prosecution. Let's assume that formal arrest and prosecution are not desired. After properly processing the shoplifter and obtaining the necessary documentation, the merchant is permitted by the civil recovery statutes to make a civil demand for the payment of a sum of money. The limits of the demand are set by the law, but the exact amount is determined by the merchant.

For example, in California the civil liability of the shoplifter is contained within Penal Code Section 490.5, which states

> When an adult or emancipated minor has unlawfully taken merchandise from a merchant's premises . . . the adult or emancipated minor shall be liable to the merchant . . . for damages of not less than fifty dollars ($50) nor more than five hundred dollars ($500), in addition to the retail value of the merchandise, if not recovered in merchantable condition . . . plus costs. An action for recovery of damages, pursuant to this subdivision, may be brought in small claims court . . . or in any other appropriate court. The provisions of this subdivision are in addition to other civil remedies and do not limit merchants or other persons to elect to pursue other civil remedies.

This California law also states that

> when an unemancipated minor's willful conduct constitutes shoplifting . . . the injured merchant may bring a civil action against the parent or legal guardian having control and custody of the minor.

The authorizing section quoted above does not require prosecution or a guilty verdict before the civil remedy can be sought, it does not set the exact amount the merchant can demand, and it does not specify the manner in which the demand must be made.

Laws such as those passed in California, Oregon, and other states have been subjected to legal scrutiny and appellate court review, and they have passed muster.

A few relatively simple procedures should be put into effect to properly utilize the civil recovery process. First, the amount of the demand should be established, and it should be uniform for everyone. Although the law does not require that the amount of money that the merchant demands be justified or explained, experience has shown that if suit is filed to recover, the court may seek an explanation of how the amount was determined. Many merchants calculate the average amount of time spent handling shoplifting cases, and they use the monetary equivalent of this amount as their demand. Others use anti-shoplifting equipment costs, which are amortized and averaged over a reasonable period of time. Whatever method is used to arrive at the amount demanded, it must be consistently applied, and it must have been arrived at by some reasonably defensible method.

Next, the shoplifter must be formally notified of the demand. It is appropriate to alert shoplifters at the time of apprehension that they may be asked to pay a civil recovery. A form letter similar to Figure 12–1 should be given to all shoplifters to alert them to the possibility of a civil recovery demand.

At some point after the apprehension, the merchant must decide whether to seek a civil recovery. On what basis is this decision made? Although we cannot set forth definitive rules for this decision, we can suggest some guidelines.

Generally, there is little sense in sending a civil demand letter to anyone who is obviously financially unable to pay the demand, for example, a homeless person, someone on welfare, or a person who is unemployed.

Date: _____

          <u>California Civil Shoplifting Remedy</u>

Name: _____

Case No.: _____

Date: _____

Dear

California Penal Code Section 490.5 authorizes merchants to seek civil damages from adult shoplifters and the parents or legal guardians of minor shoplifters. The law authorizes the retailer to recover damages of not less than $50 nor more than $500, costs and the value of the merchandise if not recovered in a merchantable condition.

The fact that _____ has either criminally prosecuted or chosen to forgo criminal prosecution does not preclude our seeking from you the civil damages allowed by law. You may receive a claim letter from us demanding &200.00 (the amount _____ has determined to represent our damages) under the provisions of California Penal Code Section 490.5. If we press our claim, you will receive a letter setting forth the full particulars and additional explanatory information.

Civil Remedy Coordinator
Security Department

Figure 12—1 Form letter notifying recipient of possible future civil recovery demand.

    With the above exceptions, all other shoplifters should be sent a civil demand letter. Merchants are advised not to pick and choose among those who do not fall within the criterion for exclusion as outlined above. All of the employed or financially secure parents of juvenile shoplifters should also be sent a letter demanding civil recovery.

    Note that merchants cannot threaten prosecution if civil demand is not paid. Such threats are criminal in nature and are strictly prohibited.

    Merchants should draft two versions of the demand letter: one for adult shoplifters (Figure 12–2) and one for the parents of juvenile shoplifters (Figure 12–3).

    All correspondence dealing with civil recovery should be sent certified mail/

10/31/90

Dear John Doe,

On 10/30/90, you were detained for the crime of theft as defined by
California Penal Code Section 484. You took, or attempted to take,
merchandise valued at $90.00 from our   store, without
making payment therefor and with the intent to convert it to your own use.

In accordance with section 490.5 of the California Penal Code, an adult
who is detained for petty theft of merchandise is liable to the merchant.
The liability is composed of (a) the retail value of the merchandise when
not recovered in a merchantable condition, (b) damages of not less than
$50.00 nor more than $500.00, and (c) costs of any necessary further legal
action.

We have analyzed our costs in dealing with these matters and determined
that $200.00 represents appropriate damages. Therefore, in accordance
with the provisions of this statute, and our rights thereunder, we
are requesting that you remit the following amount:

        Civil Damages: $ 200.00

Should you fail to make this payment by 11/14/90, a civil action will
be instituted against you in the appropriate small claims court.
Payment must be made by either cashier's check or money order made
payable to   and sent to the following
address (Please indicate the file number noted above on your payment):

Payment by you of the above amount constitutes satisfaction of only
the civil remedies   has available under California law. It does
not constitute a compromise of any criminal proceedings which may be
pending against you. A copy of the statute is attached for your reference.

Sincerely,

Civil Remedy Coordinator
Security Department

Figure 12–2   Form letter for adult shoplifters following through on civil demand.

return receipt requested. A case file should be maintained for each case, and all
correspondence and memoranda of telephone calls, conversations, or other activity
should be documented in detail in this case file.

In most jurisdictions, once a demand is made, it should be pursued to its conclusion. Merchants are advised against sending civil demand letters and dropping
the matter if no response is received or if the demand is refused. Various legal
authorities agree with the Attorney General of the State of California, who stated,
"Prudent business practice might suggest that the threat to file civil action contained
in the 'letter of demand' not be made idly or falsely without any intent to follow

10/31/90

File Number: 10/4/000/0

Dear John Doe,

On 10/30/90, John Doe, Jr., your son, an unemancipated minor,
was detained for the crime of theft as defined by California Penal Code
Section 484. Your son took, or attempted to take, merchandise valued
at $90.00 from our   store, without making payment
therefor and with the intent to convert it to his/her own use.

In accordance with section 490.5 of the California Penal Code, the parent
or legal guardian of an unemancipated minor who is detained for petty theft
of merchandise is liable to the merchant. The liability is composed of
(a) the retail value of the merchandise when not recovered in merchantable
condition, (b) damages of not less than $50.00 nor more than $500.00,
and (c) costs of any necessary further legal action.

We have analyzed our costs in dealing with these matters and determined
that $200.00 represents appropriate damages. Therefore, in accordance
with the provisions of this statute, and our rights thereunder, we
are requesting that you remit the following amount:

      Civil Damages $ 200.00

Should you fail to respond to this demand and fail to make payment by
11/14/90, an action for recovery of damages will be instituted against
you in small claims court as authorized by the statute. Payment must
be made by either cashier's check or money order made payable to
                 and sent to the following address   (Please indicate
the file number above on your payment)

Payment by you of the above amount constitutes satisfaction of only
the civil remedies   has available under California law. It does not
constitute a compromise of any criminal proceedings which may be pending
against your son. A copy of the statute is attached for your reference.

Sincerely,

Civil Remedy Coordinator
Security Department

Figure 12–3 Form letter for juvenile shoplifters following through on civil demand.

through with such an action."[1] Therefore, unless the payment is received as demanded, merchants should always file suit to collect the civil demand in an appropriate
court, which is normally a small claims court (unless, of course, the merchant has
received new information that places the wrongdoer in an excluded class).

Civil demands are frequently sent to shoplifters who are being prosecuted criminally. It is not unusual for the attorney representing an alleged shoplifter to request
suspension of the civil demand until the criminal case has been adjudicated. This

request should certainly be granted. After the criminal case has concluded, assuming the shoplifter has been found guilty, the civil demand process should be renewed. Of course, if the defendant has been adjudged not guilty, then the merchant's civil demand becomes moot, and the merchant may now face civil demands for false arrest and other torts.

Before filing a small claims (or other appropriate) court action, the merchant should give the defendant notice to that effect in writing (Figure 12–4). The use of certified mail is again recommended. An appropriate amount of time should be allowed to expire between the various steps in the recovery process; prudence suggests that at least 15 to 20 days be allowed before pursuing the next step in the collection process. Conversely, an excessive amount of time (that is, two or more months) between actions is also ill advised.

Shoplifters may agree to pay the demand but request a multiple-payment arrangement. Merchants should agree to this plan and define in specific terms the

11/22/90

Dear John Doe,

On 10/31/90, we notified you of our demand for payment of civil damages pursuant to California Penal Code 490.5. This demand resulted from your detention for theft which occurred on 10/30/90 .

As of this date, we have received no response to our demand. Should payment not be received by 12/06/90, we will immediately institute civil proceedings against you. A copy of our original letter is attached for your reference.

Sincerely,

Civil Remedy Coordinator
Security Department

Attachment

Figure 12–4 Form letter notifying recipient of intent to file in small claims court.

payment arrangements, which should then be confirmed in writing (Figure 12–5). Naturally, all payments received should be acknowledged in writing (Figure 12–6).

Small claims court procedures vary from state to state. The merchant should be represented in court by someone who is familiar with the facts of the shoplifting case, who has copies of all the documentation available for the court, and who is articulate and will be appropriately attired.

How effective is the civil demand procedure? If demands are directed at the appropriate people (that is, those who are employed or have the apparent ability to pay), a return rate of 90% is certainly not unusual. One of the authors administered a civil demand program for more than eight years, and in his experience, fewer than 4% of the cases he's seen have required a small claims suit. Even when attorneys call on behalf of clients seeking an explanation of the civil demand procedure (many attorneys have never heard of the authorizing law), payment is usually made very quickly.

The tracking and follow-up required to administer an efficient civil recovery program of some size make computerization feasible. Various commercially available software programs can be adapted to this task.

There are also commercial enterprises that will administer a civil recovery program for merchants. These businesses will handle the entire process from start to finish, or they will take control of the cases that the merchant has been unsuccessful in handling. The one aspect of the civil recovery process that these firms generally cannot do is to appear in small claims court for the merchant; in most states, small claims court procedures preclude the appearance of attorneys or surrogates.

Merchants who are interested in implementing a civil recovery program should first consult with the company attorney to ascertain whether the law is applicable in that jurisdiction and, if so, what its requirements, limitations, and procedures are.

SUMMARY

We strongly believe that civil recovery laws have helped deter shoplifting. The law's effect on deterring first offenses is difficult to assess, but experience has shown in many companies that these laws do deter repeat offenses. In our experience with one such program, not a single shoplifter repeated the offense after paying a civil penalty.

Most laws do not specify for what purpose the collected damages must be used. However, the intent of the legislatures in passing these laws is clear: The laws are intended to deter shoplifting and to assist merchants in bearing the high costs of anti-shoplifting personnel and equipment. Therefore, knowing that what the legislature can giveth, the legislature can taketh away, we strongly believe it behooves the merchant to use the funds obtained from civil recovery programs for purposes that are in keeping with the spirit and intention of the civil demand laws: to prevent shoplifting and to help defray its cost to the merchant and to the public. Merchants

10/31/90

RE: File Number 10/4/000/0

Dear John Doe,

Per your conversation with this office, I have approved a
payment schedule for you to follow. The due dates are listed
below.

12/01/90	50.00
01/01/91	50.00
02/01/91	50.00
03/01/91	50.00

200.00   TOTAL

Please make your cashier's check or money orders payable to
Security and send them to the below address:

Please list the file number above on your checks or money orders
for proper credit.

If you should have any further questions, please feel free
to call me at

Very truly yours,

Civil Remedy Coordinator
Security Department

DM:cr

Figure 12–5 Form letter outlining multiple-payment arrangement.

11/22/90

Dear John Doe,

We have received $200.00 from you as full
satisfaction of the claim asserted by our demand letter.

As a matter of information, the satisfaction of the
civil matter does not in any way affect or compromise
any criminal proceedings which may be pending against
your son.

Thank you for your attention to this matter.

Sincerely,

Civil Remedy Coordinator
Security Department

Figure 12–6 Form letter acknowledging payment.

can always have a clear conscience when appearing before a judge in small claims court if they can honestly state that the civil recovery funds are used exclusively for anti-shoplifting activities, personnel, equipment, and training. Civil recovery monies should not be put into a general fund as miscellaneous income.

Finally, a word of caution: All civil recovery programs must be administered so as to avoid claims of discrimination, deal-making, or inconsistent application. Articles about civil recovery programs always mention the potential for abuse and the "fairness" of some provisions of these laws.[2] For example, a frequently mentioned question concerns the legitimacy of laws that permit retailers to collect penalties from the parents of juveniles caught shoplifting. Shoplifters often question how the merchant arrived at the amount of the demand when flexibility is allowed. For these reasons and others, the administration of civil demand programs must be well-planned, scrupulously fair and impartial, and managed with sensitivity, good judgment, and intelligence.

NOTES

1. California Attorney General George Deukmejian in *Attorneys General Opinion* No. CR 79/9 I.L., in letter to California State Senator Newton Russell, March 1, 1979.
2. *Marin Independent Journal* (Marin County, Calif.) January 25, 1990, p. B-6, for example.

13

Extraordinary Events

Experience tells us to be prepared for the unexpected in retail security. What may commence as an ordinary shoplifting incident could result in major media attention, adverse customer relations, or exposure to a lawsuit. Extraordinary events aren't restricted to incidents in which the shoplifter is taken into custody. A person, usually a child, is sometimes returned to the store with stolen goods and the desire to confess. Retailers sometimes receive letters of conscience. The procedures for handling these events are worth examining.

It's not our intention to identify every incident that might result in a delicate or potentially explosive situation but rather to expose the reader to the broad range of extraordinary events and to offer guidelines for handling them. For each situation discussed in this chapter, it has been assumed that all of the rules set forth with respect to when and how to make an apprehension have been followed and that the security agent is absolutely certain that the suspect has in fact shoplifted. In this chapter, the following categories of extraordinary events are examined:

- VIPs
- the mentally incompetent, infirm, and ill
- shoplifters arrested by outsiders
- children returned by parents
- voluntary confessions
- complaints

VIPS

For our purposes, the very important person (VIP) usually falls into one of the following categories:

- public celebrities or public officials
- well-known community members
- "good" customers
- law enforcement officials and their relatives

Retailers obviously can't develop a different policy on how to handle the almost endless list of different VIPs. Should the spouse of a nationally renown athlete be handled any differently than a city council member? There's no need to focus that narrowly.

The apprehension of a VIP can generate an environment that becomes chaotic and confusing to the person who made the apprehension. Imagine having stopped and perhaps even handcuffed someone for theft and then discovering that it is a prominent citizen or celebrity. VIPs normally take full advantage of their status and attempt to overpower employees with their importance and influence. How the employee who made the apprehension reacts to the VIP's threats is vital to the eventual outcome of the case and the protection of the employer's interests.

The first thing the security employee must do is to secure the environment to prevent additional confusion and to avoid giving the suspect the opportunity to dispose of the stolen merchandise. Next, the security employee should call for a supervisor or manager and advise the suspect that a supervisor is responding. Security agents must resist the temptation to apologize and attempt to justify their actions. At this point, there is no need to apologize or to explain anything. The best course of action is simply to attempt to calm the situation and to await the supervisor's arrival.

Once the supervisor arrives, he or she should be taken aside beyond the VIP's hearing, and the subordinate should fully explain the observations leading up to the apprehension and the details of the apprehension itself. The apprehending employee should be able to describe the stolen merchandise and its place of concealment.

With the apprehending agent present but in the background (the agent's immediate presence and participation will obviously be a catalyst to the suspect's continued agitation), the supervisor should calmly explain to the VIP that security personnel observed the VIP taking and concealing an item of merchandise (describing the item and the area from which it was taken) and that the supervisor believes that the VIP is still in possession of the merchandise. The VIP should then be invited to relinquish the item and explain how this mistake could have been made. At this point, the fact that a theft has been committed should be minimized. The object is to obtain the stolen merchandise from the VIP in the presence of a witness.

Once the merchandise has been recovered and the VIP has offered an explanation of the incident, the supervisor can then follow company procedures with respect to the treatment of VIPs. Some companies make no distinction between VIPs and common folk with respect to prosecution; other companies may be satisfied simply to recover their goods and release the VIP. We suggest that VIPs be treated just like every other shoplifter. Store policies that are applied consistently cannot be successfully challenged as discriminatory or selective.

A word of caution: If the VIP is prosecuted, it will become a matter of public record. If a VIP is released, the fact of the apprehension must be held in confidence. Even when a VIP is legitimately apprehended and released, conversations about the incident should be avoided with people who do not have an official need to know. It is tempting for security agents or other employees to tell their friends about incidents involving VIPs, but they should resist the temptation. Such talk may not meet the legal standard of defamation, but why run the risk? The only appropriate place to discuss any apprehension, other than within the company with those who genuinely need to know, is in a court of law.

When caught shoplifting, many VIPs offer to make immediate restitution. Do not accept such offers under any circumstances. Even if you decide to release the shoplifter, do not accept money for the stolen merchandise. VIPs who really want the item should be directed to the selling floor to purchase it in the normal manner. Never accept money from a shoplifter in the security office, whether for merchandise or for any other reason.

If the VIP shoplifter is prosecuted, the booking by the police will be a public record. The media, who routinely scan booking records, may spot the booking record and call the store for details. The response depends on company policy concerning such matters, but we suggest that the response be, "No comment." The arrest record speaks for itself, and the media are not an appropriate venue in which to try the case.

"Good" Customers

How should "good" customers—that is, customers of long standing or big spenders—be treated if caught shoplifting? If the shoplifter is a true kleptomaniac, the store may make a special arrangement with the individual's family, as discussed in Chapter 2. If the shoplifter is not suffering from any mental problems, the management must decide how to resolve the incident. As we have tried to stress throughout this book, consistency is important. When dealing with the issue of shoplifting, it is imprudent to randomly select a particular individual's fate, nor should the decision be based on social status or real or potential economic gain to the business. For the most part, thought should be given to these extraordinary cases before they occur, and a policy decision should be reached well in advance of the need to apply it.

All things being equal, the shoplifter who is a "good customer" should be treated just like any other shoplifter. To look the other way simply because the individual represents a sizable volume of business is to attach an economic value to your tolerance for crime. Another consideration is how much the "good customer" may have stolen from you in the past. If you dismiss the incident casually, you send the message that those who spend a lot of money in your store are allowed to steal from it. Is this really a supportable position with which you are comfortable?

Law Enforcement Officials and Their Relatives

A vexing situation arises when an official or a relative of an official, particularly a law enforcement official, is apprehended for shoplifting. How should these people be handled? There is no easy answer to this question; management must analyze local customs, traditions, and the political realities of the community.

When a relative of a law enforcement official has been apprehended for shoplifting, we suggest that the official be notified of the event and asked for a recommendation. Occasionally, a police officer will suggest that the relative be handled just as all other shoplifters are handled. More commonly, the law enforcement officer will personally come to pick up the relative. Whatever the ultimate resolution, all normal documentation should be completed.

In the rare case when an active member of a law enforcement agency is apprehended for shoplifting, we suggest that the commanding officer be contacted immediately, apprised of the situation, and asked for a recommendation. Dealing with active law enforcement personnel in these situations requires extraordinary care and skill. Most off-duty police officers are armed, and this creates a potentially dangerous situation. Suspects should obviously be disarmed, but extreme caution, tact, and diplomacy must be used in dealing with police personnel. Additionally, the incident can be potentially devastating for these shoplifters—they will likely lose their job—and the situation is fraught with many highly charged emotional issues. The apprehension of police personnel is one of the most difficult apprehensions to handle adroitly, and planning and forethought are essential to carrying it off successfully and professionally.

THE MENTALLY INCOMPETENT, INFIRM, AND ILL

When it comes to handling mentally incompetent, infirm, and ill shoplifters, several issues are involved. People who are mentally incompetent generally cannot form the requisite intent required to commit a crime and therefore cannot be criminally prosecuted. The preferred procedure is to simply recover the stolen property and perhaps to refer the person to an appropriate treatment or care agency.

Shoplifters who are aged and infirm deserve special consideration. It is appropriate to question their motivation for shoplifting. Was the theft committed out of need? Is the person indigent or homeless? Is there any evidence that the individual is a professional shoplifter? Again, consistency is important. If aged shoplifters are to be released on their first offense, it must be made clear to them that the consequences will be much more severe if they are apprehended again. A referral to a treatment agency might be appropriate.

Shoplifters who are obviously ill at the time of apprehension deserve to be referred for treatment. Calling for an ambulance is certainly appropriate. Remember that anyone who is detained or arrested for shoplifting is your responsibility while in your custody. It may be legally improper as well as morally questionable to simply discharge an obviously ill person onto the street to fend for themselves or be victimized by others.

There is only one course of action if a detainee becomes ill, claims they are ill, or appears to be ill, and that is to summon emergency medical assistance. In some cases, agents have ignored complaints or signs of distress because they believed the illness was feigned to gain sympathy and release, only to have the shoplifter die right in the store! Such needless tragedies are invariably redressed in civil courts with awesome penalties. Aside from any punitive awards, the sensitivity to human dignity and suffering should not be lost just because a crime has allegedly been committed.

SHOPLIFTERS ARRESTED BY OUTSIDERS

On rare occasions, customers or neighboring merchants arrest someone for shop- lifting and bring them to the store from which the allegedly stolen merchandise appears to have originated. Even if the detainee admits to the theft, the store cannot accept the "prisoner" because no store employee observed the crime. The store may accept the merchandise if it's voluntarily surrendered. The detainee remains the responsibility of the person who detained him or her. What that person does to dispose of the matter—that is, call the police or release the detainee—is not the store's affair. However, the merchant should document the incident in the form of a standard report or at least a memorandum for future reference and should ensure that the merchandise is itemized in the report with proof that the goods were returned to stock, if that is the case.

CHILDREN RETURNED BY PARENTS

If the parents of a child are willing to take the time and effort to escort the youngster back to the store from which the child stole, the merchant must respond. The parents obviously wish to teach their child a lesson in the hope that he or she will learn the consequences of taking someone else's property. Unfortunately, not all parents appreciate the potential positive impact this can have. For a youngster, it is a humiliating and painful experience to be confronted by an authority figure and be obliged to hand over the stolen item or to pay compensation for the theft. It's often a tearful event.

The store's role is not so much to scold as it is to accept the apology and the return of the property and to firmly warn the young offender not to commit a crime again. The whole matter shouldn't require more than a few minutes, and it can be handled by a member of the store management or a representative from the security department. The parents should be thanked, and a brief memo should be prepared to memorialize the event, even if the names of the parties are unknown. Don't question or pursue the issue of identity with the parents.

If situations of this kind are handled properly, there may be fewer shoplifting problems in the future.

VOLUNTARY CONFESSIONS

A voluntary confession usually arrives in the form of a conscience letter and is accompanied by a money order to pay for what was taken. Every such letter we've seen has been inspired by a religious experience or conversion. Some writers are anonymous; some identify themselves. In reality, the identity of the party is not important. We've maintained a conscience letter file for years, indexing the name of the letter writer, if known. Some manner of documenting the receipt of the letter and the restitution is needed.

These letters usually identify the merchandise that was stolen. The easiest way to handle restitution is to record a sale with the restitution money in the appropriate department. This will offset the inventory shortage that was caused by the original loss. If the loss occurred in prior years, the sale will inflate the book inventory, but the consequence of that inflation will be so minuscule that it's hardly worth mentioning. More important, the money will be accounted for, and the receipt issued for the sale can be attached to the conscience letter.

If the writer is identified by name and address, a brief letter acknowledging receipt of the letter and the store's appreciation is in order.

Occasionally, shoplifters may appear at the store in person to ease their conscience by apologizing and making restitution. These instances should be handled politely with as few words as possible and an expression of appreciation. Render a receipt for the restitution or assist the individual in paying for the merchandise at the point of sale and allow the individual to retain the register receipt. Document the incident with whatever information is volunteered.

COMPLAINTS

Complaint letters help to justify our insistence on the complete documentation of all apprehensions. By reviewing the reports of the apprehension, the merchant can obtain the full facts surrounding the detention. Complaints should be handled by store managers or owners and dealt with in a forthright manner. The facts contained in the written reports should be reviewed with the complainant. Although the complainant may argue about minor details or emphasis, there should be no room for disagreement about the basic facts of the theft. The merchant's aim should be to have the complainant agree with the basic facts. Once this has happened and the complainant has admitted the theft, handling the complaint should be a downhill effort.

The approach taken should reflect politeness, concern, and sincerity, but firmness and support for the apprehension and the method in which it was handled should be the overriding tone of the conversation. Many complaint calls are simply a smoke screen designed to divert attention from the theft and to obtain some degree of leniency or diversion from normal processing.

A word of caution: Complaints should always be listened to with an open mind. Although unlikely, it is always possible that an employee or security agent has, against all directives to the contrary, embellished or otherwise falsified an apprehension report. Claims that company reports are inaccurate should be thoroughly investigated and fully resolved.

SUMMARY

Extraordinary events tend to fall into one of two categories:

1. A special person or set of circumstances is involved in an arrest.
2. Someone admits to shoplifting, and no arrest is involved.

In the former situation, upper management must usually be involved. In the latter, lower management may dispose of the matter. It would be foolhardy to attempt to develop very specific policies and procedures for the former, but written procedures may be developed for the latter.

Sound general policies and procedures can serve as the foundation for the judgment calls that management must make when faced with extraordinary events. Those judgment calls should be considered before the call is required. Managers should practice handling a variety of imaginary scenarios in preparation for similar events. How would you handle the arrest of the chief of police's juvenile child? The arrest of the pastor of the largest church in town? The mayor's spouse?

14

Court Appearance and Testimony

Sooner or later, every employee who is involved in apprehending shoplifters will be required to appear in court and testify regarding a particular apprehension in which they were involved. The courtroom demeanor of the security officer and the skill with which he or she testifies can determine the outcome of the case. Thus, knowing how to behave and present oneself in a courtroom are skills that must be mastered. Technically sound cases have been lost due to poor or marginal witnesses, and conversely, marginal cases have been won by strong and skillful witnesses. The facts of a given case, as they exist in the written formal report and in the recollection of a witness, are inert. It is the witness, and only the witness, that can breathe life into facts with oral testimony. By virtue of the trial itself, two sets of "facts" will be offered: one set by the prosecution and the other by the defense. The court or the jury will find one set more believable or credible than the other, hence the verdict of guilty or not guilty. It boils down to which witness the jury believes. The facts and the witness who offers the facts become so intermeshed that it's almost impossible to separate the two. For all intents and purposes, they become one: good witness—good facts; bad witness—bad facts.

Lay people summoned into court don't understand this; their errors in courtroom demeanor and testimony are excusable. However, security personnel are obliged to fully understand and perfect their courtroom demeanor and testimony skills as a natural and necessary part of their performance. If a witness understands the following axioms and uses them accordingly, they will serve as a basic guide for testing.

Most of this chapter comes from Sennewald, C. (1980). "Training Guidelines for Courtroom Demeanor and Testimony." In T. Walsh and R. Healy (eds.), *Protection of Assets Manual* (Santa Monica: Merritt Co.).

1. What you say is important, but how you say it can be more important. (This is a modification of the old adage, "It's not what you say, but how you say it that counts.")
2. Jurors choose to believe who they want to believe, and they tend to believe who they like.
3. Jurors tend to like or dislike others based on how they look, act, and talk.
4. The witness stand is like a stage, and the witnesses are the cast of characters.

These observations are not meant to denigrate the jury or the judicial system. They merely reflect the real world. Indeed, we believe in and respect the jury system.

COURTROOM DEMEANOR
Pretrial Preparation

Weeks and sometimes months will elapse between the scheduling of a trial and the trail date. For a witness to be articulate and confident, pretrial preparation should include the following:

- Read the file the day before the trial to refamiliarize yourself with the case.
- Read the file again on the morning of your testimony to sharpen your recollection of details such as times, locations, sequences of events, names, and who said what.
- Examine in detail any physical evidence that is to be introduced.
- Discuss the case with other witnesses who were present. This discussion should be a "walk-through" from the beginning to the end of the case. This will help intensify and clarify your recollection.
- Don't be discouraged or shocked to discover that the prosecuting attorney is totally unfamiliar with the case on the day of the trial. This unfamiliarity is usually due to the case load in the prosecutor's office. The prosecutor may pull you aside for a quick run-through, sometimes minutes before the case is called. Prepare the prosecutor by highlighting the facts. He or she will delve more deeply into the case as you unfold the facts on the stand during the direct examination.
- Be sure to read a transcript of the preliminary hearing, provided in felony cases ready for trial, because it will contain your verbatim testimony. Reading the transcript will refresh your memory about what you testified to at the hearing.
- In civil matters, follow the directions of your counselor when he or she reviews your testimony with you.

Personal Appearance and Grooming

The witness should be an impeccable picture of good grooming and dress and must look professional. Good grooming and dress include the following:

- A conservative business suit, white shirt, and conservative tie for men.
- A conservative dress or suit (not a skirt and blouse), dress shoes, and stockings for women. A minimum amount of simple jewelry should be worn.
- Hair should be clean, neatly trimmed, and conservatively styled.
- Witnesses will pass and sit relatively close to the jury. They will be able to see such details as hands, face, fingernails, and shoes. Something as small as dirty or bitten fingernails can make an unfavorable impression on members of the jury.
- If possible, carry reports and evidence into court in a briefcase or attaché case rather than in a bag or paper sack.

The Question of Fear

Witnesses dread getting on the witness stand for a variety of reasons, including a form of stage fright (facing a courtroom full or people), fear of the unknown (first time on the stand), anxiety over the cross-examination process because of having been tripped up by a defense attorney on a previous case, or fear of a judge who has a mean reputation. Fear has physical manifestations; people can see or otherwise sense fear, and it tends to cloud one's credibility, especially the credibility of a law enforcement officer or security professional. A jury understands and even sympathizes with a layperson's anxieties, but the same jury is not sympathetic to a witness whose chosen occupation requires courtroom testimony.

How can a witness overcome this fear? There's no definitive answer, but there are a number of things to do and consider:

1. Understand that even seasoned entertainers experience a mild form of fear before they go on stage. It's natural. They have learned to overcome most fear through self-determination. They have a job to do, so they grit their teeth and do it.
2. Have confidence in yourself. Take pride in the work you do and the importance of that work and recognize the importance and value of your strong testimony.
3. Anticipate how well you will do on the stand. Expect success, not failure or a problem.
4. Consider testifying a unique challenge. Very few people ever have the opportunity to testify in a court of law. The experience is one to cherish.
5. Just before going on the stand, take some deep breaths. It will get extra oxygen into your system, and it will help you think more clearly.
6. If your mouth is dry, get a drink of water before you get on the stand, and hold the water in your mouth until it's time to approach the stand.
7. Go to the public restroom. Look at yourself in the mirror. Make sure you look your best, and feel good about how you look. Feel good about yourself.

At the Counsel Table

A witness who is asked to sit with the prosecutor at the counsel table becomes a participant instead of a spectator in the proceedings. When you are sitting at the table, you are in a fishbowl; it is comparable to being on the witness stand. Your conduct at the table must be serious, objective, and businesslike.

- Only smile if the humor is appreciated by the jury.
- Don't shake your head when listening to testimony you know is untrue.
- Don't raise your eyebrows in disbelief.
- Sit erect, fold your hands, focus your attention on each witness with objective interest, and refrain from any display of emotion that could be misread by the jury.
- Bring paper and pencil with which to make notes or to communicate with the prosecutor.
- Don't write or communicate unless it's important and the prosecutor needs the information immediately.

Being Called to and Approaching the Witness Stand

When your name is called to testify, walk toward the witness stand at a brisk pace, stop somewhere short of the stand itself, and face the court bailiff or clerk. The bailiff will be standing and waiting to administer the oath. Raise your right hand. The oath is phrased in the form of a question to which you reply, "I do."

- Speak loudly enough for the jury to hear.
- Speak clearly and with conviction.
- Proceed to the chair in the witness stand, sit down comfortably but in a businesslike posture (sit erect, cross your ankles, fold your hands on your lap), and adjust the microphone (if there is one) to several inches from your mouth.

Body Language on the Witness Stand

There is much to be said about body language on the stand. Body language (nonverbal communication) is another form of testimony. Recommended behavior includes the following:

- Don't slide down or slouch in the chair.
- Never fold your arms across your chest.
- Avoid nervous habits or characteristics such as playing with your hair, scratching, or picking at your fingernails.
- Don't frown or stare at the defendant.
- Don't glower at the defense attorney, even if the defense attorney glowers at you.
- Don't maintain a stone face; be naturally responsive.
- Don't sit with one foot up on the other knee.

- Keep your hands folded on your lap in a relaxed fashion.
- Seek opportunities to smile genuinely.
- Watch the attorney frame the question. Begin the answer first looking at the attorney, then looking over to the jurors as you talk, making eye contact with two or three of them.
- Look over or up to the judge from time to time, particularly while he or she is speaking.
- Do have confidence in yourself and your mission. It shows whether you do.

THE PROCESS OF TESTIMONY

In criminal cases, the People present their case first. In civil cases, the plaintiff goes first. Let's take the criminal case as an example and follow the process of testimony with the first witness called to the stand.

Direct Examination

After the witness had given his name, address, employer, occupation, and area of responsibility in that occupation, the prosecutor usually sets the stage that will lead to the heart of the witness's testimony, for example, "Were you on duty during the early afternoon of July 23, 1990?" Then come the open-ended questions, such as, "Tell us what happened?" The witness then narrates the events, usually with few or no interruptions (from the prosecutor at least) until the entire story is told. The prosecutor's supportive role is apparent by her acceptance of the testimony, and the witness is encouraged from time to time by such questions as, "And then what happened?" During the direct examination, the defense counselor may not ask any questions, but he does have the right to object to testimony that in his judgment falls outside the rules of evidence.

Evidence

Black's Law Dictionary defines evidence as "that which tends to prove or disprove any matter in question, or to influence the belief respecting it; that which tends to furnish proof." There are many categories of evidence: admissible, inadmissible, direct, indirect, circumstantial, conclusive, corroborative, cumulative, documentary, expert, hearsay, opinion, parol (oral testimony), physical, prima facie, relevant, and many others. Only a few of these categories are of general concern. Most are of legal and technical concern to the attorneys and the court.

Admissible Evidence

Physical evidence is any tangible item pertinent to the case that was legally obtained. Physical evidence is introduced at the trial by the testimony of the witness who obtained it. For example, stolen merchandise that was recovered from the shoplifter at the time of apprehension and retained in evidence would be introduced as physical evidence by the person who recovered the merchandise. This physical evidence would support the claim that a theft had taken place.

Oral evidence, or *testimony,* is the verbal statement by a witness under oath of everything pertinent to the case at hand that was perceived by the witness through sight, hearing, or other senses. Testimony is the most common type of evidence given by security personnel or store employees involved in shoplifting apprehensions.

Documentary evidence consists of written materials, such as apprehension reports, that are pertinent to the case at hand. Documentary evidence is similar to physical evidence in that it is normally introduced by the person who prepared the report or other documents.

Inadmissible Evidence

The term *inadmissible evidence* is an oxymoron because information or items that are inadmissible are not evidence. Witnesses often make the mistake of attempting to testify to information that is legally not allowed. Inadmissible testimony includes opinions (unless the witness has been accepted as an expert witness), conclusions, and hearsay (what someone other than the defendant said). Witnesses may testify about what they saw, heard, and did, but not about their opinion or conclusion about the admissible evidence. Witnesses may only testify to facts that they know or believe to be true. Hearsay is not allowed as evidence because the court, the jury, and the defendant are entitled to hear testimony directly from the people who said it so that they can evaluate their credibility, subject them to cross-examination, and evaluate the information and its source for themselves.

Cross-Examination

When the prosecutor is satisfied that her witness has presented all the facts, she turns the witness over to her adversary for cross-examination, usually by making the statement, "Your witness." Now the adversary aspects of the trial begin. The defense attorney is in charge of the witness and poses all of the questions. The line of questioning must be germane to the testimony already given. He normally requests that the witness reiterate some of his earlier testimony, or he will restate some of the testimony as a preface to a question, or both. For example, the defense attorney might say, "You testified you first saw the defendant 'around' two o'clock in the afternoon. I'm not sure I understand what 'around' means. Could you tell us if it was before or after two o'clock?"

There are three key differences between direct examination and cross-examination.

1. A witness is obviously on the offense during direct examination but is on the defense during cross-examination.

2. A witness will speak more during direct examination, whereas the defense attorney will speak more during cross-examination.
3. The witness is "asked" for answers on direct examination, but is "directed to answer" questions while on cross-examination, at least from the witness's perspective.

When the defense attorney is satisfied that he has exhausted his probe and has perhaps raised some question or doubt about the witness's original story with the jurors, he terminates his cross-examination by advising the court, "I have nothing further."

Redirect Examination

Following cross-examination, the witness is not necessarily finished. The prosecutor may want to amplify an issue that was raised by the defense, or the testimony may have triggered a new thought that she wants explored.

Recross-Examination

Each time the prosecutor examines her witness, the defense is entitled to cross-examine the testimony just offered. There are usually no more than four examinations for each court appearance, although one of the authors underwent eight examinations when there was more than one defendant in a trial and each had his own attorney.

When both sides have exhausted their questions and the testimony is concluded, the judge dismisses the witness by saying, "You're excused." This is the signal to leave the witness stand after saying, "Thank you, Your Honor."

TESTIMONY

The first words a witness speaks from the stand will be his full name and address. As a rule the clerk will ask the witness to spell out the last name, for example, "Constance B. Koskovick, K-o-s-k-o-v-i-c-k-, 49211 Davenport Street, Omaha, Nebraska." If a court reporter (a stenographer) is present, she will look directly at you as you spell your name to ensure that it is recorded accurately. If a court reporter is present, speak to her but bear in mind that the court clerk is also recording the information. If there is no reporter, speak to the clerk.

Consider the following points while testifying on the witness stand:

- Make sure that everyone can hear you.
- Clearly articulate all words so that they are understood.
- Don't speak rapidly; speed tends to run words together.
- Remember, you're on stage, and everyone is focusing on you.

- Answer each question directly. Don't edit or volunteer added information.
- Don't qualify answers with the word *but*.
- Don't be too quick to answer every question. Consider what you're going to say before you say it. A pause will allow for objections.
- If an objection is raised, stop your testimony until the court rules. The court will either sustain (agree with) the objection or overrule (disagree with or deny) the objection. If an objection is sustained, the question may not be answered. If an objection is overruled, the question may be answered.
- Don't answer a question with a question.
- If you don't understand a question, say so.
- If you don't know the answer to a question, say so.
- If you don't remember, say so.
- If your mouth becomes dry and it's difficult to speak, ask for a glass of water.

Things to Avoid

Every occupation has its own glossary of terms, pet phrases, jargon, and slang, none of which has a place in testimony. The same is true for profanity. If you want the jury to hear and to understand you, speak their language. Avoid referring to time in military/police terminology. Commonly used phrases such as *busted, burned, he made me*, and *conducting an S.O.* (stake-out or surveillance) will only confuse or turn off jurors.

While on the stand, you should say, "Yes sir" and "No sir" or "Yes ma'am" or "No ma'am," "Mr. Green" (not "defendant" or "suspect"), and "Your Honor."

Never carry or display any weapons, handcuffs, or other such devices while outside or inside the courtroom. Being seen with these items could prejudice the jury and hence affect the outcome of your case.

Security personnel should be cautious in what documents, reports, and notes they take to the stand with them. In most jurisdictions, the defense counsel is entitled to see in its entirety any document referred to or examined by a witness in the course of testimony. Company counsel or the prosecuting attorney should be consulted regarding the presence or use of any documents during testimony. It may be desirable to have certain case notes that can be used to refresh your memory; however, the details should be discussed with and approved by counsel in advance.

The Adversary Attorney

An adversary attorney in a security professional's world is a defense attorney in criminal matters and usually the plaintiff's attorney in civil matters. In criminal and civil cases, an attorney's task is to make the best possible case for the client. As a rule, judgments for the plaintiff, an acquittal, or a not-guilty verdict measure success. To achieve success, attorneys adopt a strategy. Part of the strategy usually includes attacking the credibility of adversary witnesses. Exposure of deception, bias, dishonesty, misconduct, or "unfair" conduct (all dealing with personal behavior) could seriously jeopardize the credibility of adversary witnesses. Common examples of each behavior follow:

- Deception: entrapment, altering facts, or fabricating facts to fill in voids or blanks.
- Bias: prejudice against the defendant's race, sex, or age or political, philosophical, or sexual orientation or a personal dislike for the defendant.
- Dishonesty: theft of the defendant's property or money at the time of the arrest or theft of part of the evidence.
- Misconduct: use of profanity during or following the arrest, use of unnecessary physical force, or sexual harassment.
- "Unfair" conduct: not letting the accused go to the toilet when asked, not letting the accused take necessary medication, or not heeding the accused's plea that minor children are alone in the car in the parking lot.

Any one of the points above could seriously undermine a security practitioner's credibility as a professional, alienate a jury, and lose the case.

One particular question that is frequently used by defense attorneys and which generates great anxiety with witnesses is, "Prior to your testimony today, have you ever discussed this case or your testimony with the prosecuting attorney or anyone else?" It is entirely probable and proper that witnesses will review their testimony with their supervisors, company counsel, or the prosecutor's office. There is no unfavorable inference to be drawn from an affirmative answer to this question. Actually, a negative answer will be immediately pursued by the defense attorney in an effort to impeach you.

Another tactic in the strategy to erode your credibility is to confuse, anger, or embarrass you. Anything that might cause you to lose composure while on the stand is tried. Following is a list of common adversary counselor's tactics with suggestions for witnesses to deal with such tactics:

Counselor accuses you of having a personal interest in the case:

You would personally like to see Mr. Schultz convicted, wouldn't you?

Response: "I have a professional, not personal, interest in this case."

Counselor points out inconsistencies between your testimony and another security employee who was with you:

Your associate testified that Mr. Schultz made five or six phone calls from the pay phone prior to going into the jewelry department. In your testimony you say Mr. Schultz made three calls. How many calls did he make, or do you even know?

Response: "To the best of my recollection he made three calls. He may have made more. My view was sometimes blocked by customers. My associate was watching the phone from a different vantage point." (Small inconsistencies are not uncommon. The point is to not get rattled and to testify only to what you know and recall.)

Counselor demands a yes or no answer to a question that really requires more detail:

> Did you rip Ms. Schultz's blouse off her back, leaving the upper portion of her body exposed to all the customers in the mall? Answer yes or no.

Response: "Inadvertently, yes sir." (You must answer each question the best way you can and rely on the court to support your right to do so. In this example, the one additional word is necessary and critical. To have attempted to answer by saying, "She was kicking me and trying to run . . . I was reaching . . . " would have been unresponsive to the question and stopped.

Counselor accuses the witness of mistreating the defendant:

> Isn't it a fact, Ms. Green, that after Ms. Schultz refused to sign your so-called statement form you got up from behind the desk, walked around to Ms. Schultz, and without a word took your right hand and forced—banged—her head into the wall?

Response: "No sir, that is not a fact." (Calmly deny all false allegations.)

Counselor asks belligerent and demeaning questions in an aggressive manner:

> You enjoy arresting women using violence and body contact, don't you, Ms. Green?

Response: "I abhor violence and do everything I can to avoid it." (The key is to remain calm and not lose composure. A simple "no" answer to that compound question (two questions in one) would have encouraged the counselor to ask, "Oh, you don't enjoy making arrests?" The trap is set because if your answer is you do enjoy arresting people it could subtly suggest that you are a sadist.

Counselor implies you're a sadist:

> You enjoy arresting people, don't you?

Response: "I like my job as an investigator. Making arrests is part of the work." Or, "I take pride in my ability to detect theft, but it's not fun to make arrests, if that's what you mean."

Counselor attempts to upset you by purposely mispronouncing your name, rank, etc.

> Now let's see, Miss Beane (name is actually Green), you say you called the police at 5:00 P.M. Is that correct?

Response: "Yes sir." (Just ignore these tactics.)

Counselor deliberately errs in repeating your earlier testimony:

> Now if I recall correctly, you testified you called the police at 4:00 P.M. They arrived at your office at 5:20 and left the office with Ms. Schultz at about 6:15 P.M. Is that correct?

Response: "No sir. I testified I called the police at 5:00 P.M., not 4:00 P.M." (Always listen carefully when a counselor is repeating your testimony. Correct errors politely.)

Counselor points out an error in your earlier testimony:

> You testified you received the original information about the alarm failure due to bypassing on Wednesday, March 6, just prior to noon. I'd like to point out that March 6 was a Thursday, not a Wednesday. Was it the sixth, or was it Wednesday?

Response: "I'm sorry, my mistake. It was March 6, a Thursday. (If indeed an error was made, freely admit it.)

Counselor rapidly fires questions at the witness, attempting to rush answers.

Response: Don't be rushed. You can't be forced to speak until you're ready. Remain calm. The adversary attorney must follow the pace you set.

Counselor repeatedly asks the same or almost the same question.

Response: Repeat the same answer, and don't show annoyance in your voice or expression.

Counselor stands in silence after the witness has answered a question and stares at the witness.

Response: Quietly wait for the next question. If the stare becomes unnerving, look elsewhere—to the rear of the courtroom, to your attorney, back to the adversary counselor—but remain silent.

AFTER GIVING TESTIMONY

You may leave the witness stand when the magistrate excuses you. Thank the magistrate with a smile, rise, and briskly walk out of the courtroom (unless of course you're obliged to set at the counsel table). By leaving the courtroom, the jury will notice your lack of personal curiosity about the outcome of the trial. You had a job to do, you did it, you have other important things to do, and the final adjudication of the issue before the court rests with those so charged, not you.

When the case is finally submitted to the jurors, they will retire to the jury room to deliberate the case. They will indeed talk about you and what you had to say. What will they think and say?

SUMMARY

An integral part of shoplifting detection is the need for the agent to subsequently testify as a percipient witness. The ability of the agent to orally convey to the jury or tribunal the sequence of events is paramount to the ultimate success of the case. Care must be taken in preparing for the testimony. The witness's appearance and deportment on the stand are as important as the facts themselves. That's also true with the agent's conduct at the counsel table and in the courthouse hallway. The actual examinations by counsel should be handled in a calm and professional manner, and every question must be answered truthfully irrespective of how potentially damaging the answer may be.

Index